Richard Eberhart
THE LONG REACH

New & Uncollected Poems
1948-1984

D1542151

A NEW DIRECTIONS BOOK

Grateful acknowledgment is made to the editors and publishers of books and magazines in which some of the poems in this collection first appeared: *American Poetry Review; From A to Z: 200 Contemporary American Poets* (The Swallow Press/Ohio University Press); *The Bellingham Review; The Chicago Tribune; Conjunctions; Cumberland Poetry Review; Chocorua* (Nadja Press); *The Devil's Millhopper; Florida Poems* (Konglomerati Press); *Forum; Four Poems* (Palaemon Press, Ltd.); *Gryphon; Harvard Magazine; High Country News; Kentucky Poetry Review; A Local Muse; The London Times Literary Supplement; Mid-Century American Poets* (Copyright 1950 by John Ciardi); *Nadja Press; National Forum; Negative Capability; New American Review; New England Review; New Poems by American Poets* (Ballantine Books); *New Hampshire/Nine Poems* (Pym-Randall Press); *New Republic; The New York Times; New York Quarterly; Paideuma; PN Review; Ploughshares; Poems to Poets* (Pomegranate Press); *Penmark Rising; Poetry Now; The Prosery; The Pomegranate Press* (broadside); *Pulse (The Lamar Review); For Rexroth (The Ark 14*, Festschrift); *I. A. Richards: Essays in His Honor* (Copyright © 1973 by Oxford University Press); *The Southern Review; Survivors* (Boa Editions); *Tamarisk; The Tiger's Eye; Vanderbilt Poetry Review; Wonders: Writing and Drawings for the Child in Us All* (Copyright © 1980 by Rolling Stone Press).

The following poems were included in the collection *Florida Poems* (Copyright © 1981 by Richard Eberhart), published by Konglomerati Press, P. O. Box 5001, Gulfport, Florida 33737: "Transformation," "Opposition," "Incidence of Flight," "The Swinging Bridge," "Mistaken Identity," "The Great Trees," "Ichetucknee," "Gainsville Sun," "Key West."

Manufactured in the United States of America
First published clothbound and as New Directions Paperbook 565 in 1984
Published simultaneously in Canada by George J. McLeod, Ltd., Toronto

Library of Congress Cataloging in Publication Data
Eberhart, Richard, 1904–
    The long reach.
    (A New Directions Book)
    I. Title.
PS3509.B456L6 1983   811'.52   83-23746
ISBN 0-8112-0885-0
ISBN 0-8112-0886-9 (pbk.)

New Directions Books are published for James Laughlin
by New Directions Publishing Corporation,
80 Eighth Avenue, New York 10011

Contents

O N E

T W O

T H R E E

∼§ O N E §∼

Chant of the Forked Lightning

Let us break the cities down
Through pulses' feel
To a metaphysical town
Where love is real.

By the sweeping sea
Of old Mont St. Michel
Eat a weeping tea
For all that's gone: allons

By the rattling Bear
Sleep in the arms of Psyche,
A diamond on the finger,
And suit of a faun.

By the eternal Zoo
Hear the murderous caw
And upshot of it all,
Give a hand to how-de-do.

Go to the babbling spring ferns
They are learning
And on the mountain tops
The ice is burning.

Go to the shark sea shoals
Where the fight's on;
And back to pastures new
Where the fable's done.

Go to the fork of lightning
In the fork of lightning lie,
To that holy hierarchy
Of what you'll ever, never be.

Passage

Time as something concrete, like the wash of a wave
    Over a sea wall.
Is not time always coming on and over us?

Time! From the Leakey skull in the Rift Valley
    Has it not always been coming over us?

Not people, not events so much as time itself,
Abstract time as if not abstract, but concrete

Time! It rushed over us when we were striplings,
Over us in mid-life, over us in age.

Time the smacker without a grudge.
It is in the air surrounding my fingers,

It is in my mind in my skull,
It is in my legs walking and my voice talking,

Sightless time! What a sightless time we have.
We can't see it, but we feel it all the time.

Ur Burial

Reach me a blue pencil of the moon,
The double-reined rings from tombs of Ur,
The lyre, the javelins from Sumer,
"The Ram caught in a thicket."

A gold dagger, a golden toilet case,
The gold helmet of Meskalam-dug;
Rein-ring and mascot from
Queen Shub-ad's chariot.

I will drink a narcotic rich and dark.
I will lie down by my master in his sarcophagus,
All our company will join in sleep
To serve the sun in a life beyond sleep.

There Is an Evil in the Air

There is an evil in the air
Like shapes of powerful phantasies
Will wheel, will snap the trees;
It is the future, terrible, everywhere.

There by the cicada-sounding sycamore;
By the mill, off the hill
Comes the power to tear and kill
Into the heart of mankind more and more.

O dreadful evil, dreadful absolute
And furious thrashing words in the heart,
From the ramparts of art triumphant, I'll
The pure cold realms of death salute.

A Man of Sense

Evil was dangled in front of him like an apple,
A winesap. He saw the apple-crush in the cider mill
Like the mesh of blossom on the trees; draining off
More evil as the amber oozed, he would drink it down,
Becoming a part of the blossom and the fruit;
So surely the wine went back to earth in him.

He became aware of evil in the very air,
In time, and while he breathed the delight of June,
He knew not what to make of the evil of the air.
Things screen us; books do; museums filled with art,
The rich success of shale-stood city towers;
War's bloody hiatus, its true or demented dreams.

To live in luxury, to love the difficult,
And clarify the ways of man to men in thought,
Perturbed by God and evil, but letting them be,
Was what the world allowed him, a special plane,
Genius for friendship with the deft and debonair,
But not to go mad over inscrutability.

Imagination was that formative intelligence
That shaped him less to action than to contemplation;
Imagination it was, the inexhaustible source,
That blessed him in luminous, suspended swirls.
He was the recipient of the ages' thought.
He knew the pleasure of an antique loss.

To a man of meditation the memorable
Makes the marmoreal; skunk cabbages can too.
He is the defender of the library cults;
Cut off from agriculture, and from locomotion
In a sense, his eye distills the fluctuant scene,
And he can be the farmer of Horace undebited.

He is for pure merriment and for pure fun.
A cynical joke with a lavender tinge, or an

7

Irish bull a yard long, or minuscule bombast in
Disruption of the over or the underdog
Infect the air with his suitable laughter.
Laughter is innocence where before there was none.

Precisely he is mysterious, but offends no man;
Talents he has, that is to have no talent unduly.
He averts from his gaze the awkward, the ugly,
A triumph of sheer character; if he is favored
It is because the times allowed an elegant fate.
Somebody else made the money, he made the manners.

To be fervent, he thought, is not to be true.
To be detached, the observer, is to be true.
The spectator of life is superior to the actor;
The actor, embroiled, does not control the action.
An impersonal eye controls its speculation,
Losing, apparently, the illusion it is in.

He triumphed, delicately, and walked along the Charles.
The old airs of Paris hung about his head.
There was no use doing anything about man.
In China the rice was coming up again.
The boats turned and curved upon the water
Not knowing the mathematical lines they were making.

He thought of poetry, and of St. John the Divine;
He thought he had known, one time, as index,
The voluminous interstices of the Inferno,
The Purgatorio, and lessly the Paradiso.
It was not this that was to be his guide.
It was a dream, a secret, a pure idea in time.

He was not a clear soul;
Clarity, perforce, was juvenile.

Often he had thrown himself away
To be sure he was not there to stay.

Espousing the inextricable
Made his temerity immiscible.

He sought in everything quality,
Which deviates into policy.

Every action involves criticism
For not being another action.

And every criticism is an instinct
For being in the inner self.

And every effort is a struggle
To evaluate and predict.

And every man loves and loses
In the guilt of experience.

He would not accept any definition of taste
Knowing that change was certain to violate it.
To live in a fluid ambience of the possible
Brought him joy; he gave it back the tentative.

To evade the substratum of one's life,
Those fixed and barnacle-encrusted pilons,
Was not a linguistic feat, but a conceptual.
Water can look like air; disturbed, it becomes flighty.

He had rejected the romantic, as was expected.
Time was when he gorged on gorgeous effect
And never understood, so stuffed, the spectacle.

What then one could not command or do
One said time's perspective would surely show.
That devil of lovers would ruin and debase

An ancient menace which exalted to confound.
At least time would make plain the issue,
Time tragedian become time comedian.

But see his corpse in the ground,
Be sure some massive stain will adhere to it.

But see his soul ascend,
Be sure in the air he will not quite see it.

The very present world was pat.
A classicist. He could get along with that.

If this was to be classical,
To accept a golden evenness
And ease the tension off the eyelids,
Order the blood, be well balanced,

He approved a modern classical stance
And thought, by St. George, that he had it.
Certain dragons of recalcitrant years
He had conquered, and was glad of it.

It was his doughtiness to imagine pure harmony,
Holding the past in fee, the future not fearing,
Walking by water of suicides, swimmers, and sailors,
Dealing out his rich increase on the air
In private meditation: a whole man,
Wholeness describing imaginary society.

If it was Athens he thought he was in,
It was cool and clean, knowledge after tragedy,
And if the ideal Christian commonwealth
It was a prized and inner unity,
And if it was the actual world he was walking in
He made it in his senses by imagination free.

Dusty Answer

Staring into dust of TV race track,
The racer almost blinded at the curve,
It was the curve of the earth,
No matter who would win or lose.

Staring into dust
Of a storm system developing a tornado,
Another kind of indeterminate looking,
From which one might be alive or dead.

Staring into the dust of a sarcophagus,
Say Egyptian, three thousand years old,
Was best of all, sufficiently mere,
Like looking at my own hand.

Old Memory

Once when I was young I bicycled
From Cork to Bantry Bay. I was in Ireland,
Young, vigorous, in love with life and Ireland.
I took a room for the night, was ushered

Up cavernous steps to a high, small chamber
Without light but a candle in the dark.
I saw the bleeding heart of Jesus, the only
Sight. Fear seized me in this foreign place.

I was pierced with recognition, heart-shatter,
Terrified, and hoped to lose consciousness.

Slant Angle

The beautiful sight is golden,
How it is all transfigured,
The dead, stiff, pale-brown blossoms
Standing up through snow in zero January

Suddenly, suddenly, because the sun
Has changed, has remarkably changed position
The dead flowers are all atint with gain
Of afternoon sun hurtling across the snow.

Words cannot come flashing fast enough
For immediacy of revelation. Etched,
Relentless, before my vision instantaneous
Winter sun on dead flowers, golden, made new.

Midwinter

I cannot go out to my study
To search for perfection,
Invite the Muses, search the past,

Because I have to stick paper
(Not to write on, written by cold)
In the door to keep out the cold.

It is twenty below. Twenty below
Would kill you if it could, but man
Knows to contrive life likelihood.

I used to shout paeons to the world,
Receive it as a blessing from the North,
Having animal spirits to delight in it.

Twenty years later no doubt no wiser
I do not want to walk into the cold,
I have lost one of my heavy gloves.

I think of the drama of sitting by the fire
Hoping the furnace will not go off,
Vaguely glad it is not going down to forty.

Lay on wood, keep the poker handy,
Thank Ben Franklin for inventing his stove,
Meditate, invite the philosophers.

Discovery

Discovery, discovery of the wild kingdom,
Lurks across the page at the end of the line,
Discovery, finally, leaps off the lines.

In between is the transience of what we do,
The tenacity of belief of what joy is, joy
In those capable of joy, hatred in the hating,

Structures coming down from Machiavelli,
Yet serene strengths in St. Theresa, St. Francis,
Are you as good? Is anybody as good as these?

Poetry survives a hurricane, yet as I write
Hundreds are dead who are unable to be distinguished
From deaths by hurricanes of earlier times.

The young come up with their lacy grace,
Who do not know as do their elders, but who
Keep intransigent strangeness impossible to put down,

They the generative, the throwers off of the old,
The young severely caught in the same complexities,
Discovery, discovery of the wild kingdom.

The Block

The sky was fair and distinct.
The trees radiated energy.
There was a sense of the eternal
In the light of the afternoon.

It is as if the world were
Wordless, absolute in itself,
Needed not the language of man.
This great world and light were true.

But I am writing this poem! This is the block,
I am blocked off from the truth and the real
Because I am mortal and because I feel.

I cannot hope to get to the truth
Of the eternal light of the afternoon
Because block out is blackout, I
Know the dictionary fails my drift.

I would say some stupendous word
It is not given man to say. Instead,
I will go and teach a class in poetry,
I will tell the young to evade perfection.

Mind

I thought the mind was high, up there,
It commanded the universe.
I thought my words would be avid,
Then averred they should be terse.

The words could not flex wings
As air became too rare
To support their flighty impetus.
I thought I should not dare.

More daring to be low and ranked
Where fellows never need the truth
But live in the realm of the real
With love and hate, joy and ruth.

This was better, I thought, and felt
A surge of fallen humanity
But when I went with them I cringed
Because I was not truly free.

In this dilemma I was caught,
Not knowing what to do
But make poems I deemed holy
For dreamers new and few.

Somewhere Else

Passion, too intemperate,
Goes off the track.
Reason, too reasonable,
Is tacky.

Where do we go from here?
Reason, too much, extreme
Passion, too much;
Lurch toward the Golden Mean.

Lurch toward the Golden Mean?
One should
Approach it gingerly,
As if an Absolute Good.

How could it be,
With lust for killing,
An Absolute Good
In disasters of our willing?

If saint and sinner are one,
The human condition is
Balanced. On one side contrition,
On one side derision.

I bow out.
If anybody has seen the light
He will bow out.
The light is beyond criticism.

The light is beyond distinction,
It is beyond division,
It is beyond question,
It is beyond precision.

Grip of the Cold

Handclasp Winter, the grip of the cold.
Severe brotherhood, put on wool or you'll freeze.
The animals will save you. Let them surround you.

Zero or forty below will kill you
If you don't watch out. Love but evade the cold,
The cold a threat embracing.

That cold kiss and embrace of New Hampshire Winter!
It wants to love you so much it will destroy you,
Walk into it covered by overcoat and fur.

The grip of freezing zero teaches us respect
For nature greater than man, man the lesser,
If he rebels nature will slice him.

It is the Winter solstice, the shortest day, Lucy's day,
The dynamic of the cold. Survive
By intelligence not to be outdone by threat,

The cold seeking the bone. The great cold indifference
To the warm heart beating in the chest against it.
Mankind will not give in to the imperviousness of Winter.

The grip, the cold. I grip you with my hand,
This cunning instrument that has defeated you
For millennia, and lived to see the Spring.

Winter, you want to kill me, but I desist,
I have a love-hate relationship with you.
I put on wool. I walk into you with impertinence.

Winter, killer. Let me force a fantasy,
I fantasize that I master you. Wind-chill me.
I salute your memory in the sweat of Summer.

Rain

The rain is alive with ancient symmetries.
It is a god of the air that on my head,
My shoulders, my hips and my feet
Blesses with care and refreshment,

Soul of my soul, ultimately unknowable,
The rain is alive as an animal
As I am alive as an animal, and we
Share reality and share mystery,

The mystery of duration and of time
That is timeless after we shall end,

The sense as infinite while we have being.
Then rain shall fall on others, enfolding them.

The Ideal and the Real

The word that burned into a page
Destroyed time, but the page is still there,
 Blank.

It was so immediate it flew away,
But reality was reality when I was young,
 Singing.

When I was young I destroyed time
While lovingly I was discovering it.
 Flashing.

I knew the absolute of the immediate
When I looked at a lily in the thicket.
 Heaven.

I knew nothing of heaven but of earth,
Earth was heaven at eye and fingertips.
 Unforgettable.

How could I know that I was obliterating time
Only that time should smudge the vision?
 Unsuspected.

The word I wrote on a page was absolute.
Everything was poetry, everything was real.
 Sensation!

The word burned into a page
That withstood the passion of my imagination,
 Another reality.

There was no death in the incredible garden,
Now age brings time on an open page,
 Inditing.

The timeless gives over to the labors of time,
Man's glimpse of perfection meets imperfection.
 Kingdom come.

Shiftings

The whole thing is seen from a
    different distance.

You thought you would have command
    of a situation,

But your brain explodes the whole of life
    As impossible to you.

You are being passed off the boards by time,
    Somebody else lives.

The enormity of the situation is perceived.
    You are rocked.

You thought you belonged to the living,
    And conducted life,

But the truth is that you belong to the dead,
    Everybody does.

So what if they make war, or make love,
    What is the difference?

You were deceived by evidence of the ego,
    I am capable.

You were no more capable than Nero,
    A fool who died.

You saw the sublimity of the absolutes,
    You won't outlast Plato.

As a matter of fact life is quixotic,
    Has ecstasies and shambles.

When you knew glory it fled,
    When pain, it left.

The desperate thing is to die,
    Because we lived.

Love Poetry

Light poems of love, love poems of light,
These I would hand-make, these indite.

I rust and die when I cannot write.
To write is to raise the sword of life-fight.

A light poem of love, a poem of light
Lets all lovers reflect delight.

Saps and juices bespeak Spring's might,
But for timeless love, let Spring alight

From Heaven knows where, and dart
Among the juices lightly to the heart.

Then love can vanquish melancholy,
The light and the love deprive folly.

Episode

The rattler dozed in the sun,
Just out of a rock overhang.
He was as natural
As the rock and himself.

A poet came along
And looked at him.

He recognized the danger.
He recognized the necessity.

The snake was about to strike.
The poet was about to write a poem.

A 3 x 5 Poem

This poem is limited
By form.
The form is 3 x 5
Homer is left out.
So is Shakespeare.

In 3 x 5
You might say the word love
And that includes everything.
Love 3 x 5,
Diminution by form.

It is classically exact.
Gargantua was gross.
A love 3 x 5
Emits control,
Omits Big Bang.

Poem of the Least

To get it down to the least
The poem should say something,
It should say zero.

The poem cannot escape
Zero saying something,
Total affront of the world.

The Scale

Does the moon feel a barb?
Do the planets feel our space probes?
No, we feel our own barbs,
We feel our own probes.

It is not love of space, nor love of time
We should enjoin
But love of our kind, mankind,
Felt in the groin.

Man unkind, or man blind,
Woman, the mother,
We should adhere to,
Woman the lover.

If we inhabit space
It may be a fine place
But we will still be looking
Into the human face,

And if we change time
It will be unbelievable
Because, though extended,
Only mortality is believable.

Let the moon alone,
Let the planets endure,
Love is of the flesh,
Let it atone.

To Alpha Dryden Eberhart:
On Being Seventy-five

When you were in high school, in the old red brick
Building, a bomb in the form of a firecracker
Went off under your seat in the schoolroom. The
Teacher thought you were the culprit, you were
Summoned and you were expelled, although your sense
Of fairness to a friend kept you from telling
That another had set off the report. Then up rose
Our fair and gentle mother, roused to go before
The school committee to attest that her son was
Not a bad boy. Bravo for her. It took courage,
But she stood by you as a youth of good character,
No revolutionary. Over half a century later
I recall this prank, its gusto, and the high sense
Of life that inhered in you and in our mother.

Another memory, when we used to go down in the meadow
Somewhere near the river, and snare gophers. We had no
Sense of their pain or of our injustice. We were boys
Out for sport. A circle of string was placed over the hole,
Run back maybe thirty feet and there on our bellies
We youths would wait for a long time for an unwary head
To pop up into sight. Zing, and we would strangle the creature,
Stand up and swing him around our heads in gusty triumph.
Then we would skin him and nail him to a board and
Salt him, and in a while have a number of such trophies.

To the Mad Poets

Happy are the mad for they are able
To see
That stones are light
That clouds are heavy
That women are men
And men are women.

Happy are these madmen
To see
That they were misbegotten
That they are misshapen
That they are free
Where others are chained.

Happy is their ferocity
Bought with painful recognition
In august cognition,
In terrible degree.
It is a happiness
Of spontaneity.

Happy are these times
To see
These madmen produced by them.
In guts and rubble of events
As from Islamic tents
They rush forth in their Fantasia.

Horsed under the maddest moon
Of ancient Africa
Rushing beyond the law
They shoot off their guns
In an ecstasy of Fantasia,
Resolving every dilemma.

Target

I tried to say the truth
But the truth kept going away.
It always belonged to somebody else,
It kept refusing to belong to me.

This got up my fighting spirit
As I said, the truth belongs to me,
I will show it to you, listen to me,
I have the truth locked in my pocket.

If I did not have the truth of the ancients
I would not have the truth of the present.
Present people who have no past, not free,
Are not people who are built to last.

Somebody is taking away the past
Thinking that there is only the present.
These, deluded by the gaudy, flaunt
Memorials that break down the next day.

I think my truth is hard as metal
And that it contains the past and present.
Nails are not used in coffins anymore
Because people insist on being cremated.

They are thus translated instantly
By fire to air and do not exist
Except to insist that there is neither
Present, past, nor future ether either.

The plain, unboxed truth, is that if we molder
Slowly, or become air by fire, we are breathed in
As ancestors by our unprotesting descendants,
They have us, and we have them, truth to see.

The Fig That Floats

He was not quite serious with women. The fig
Of Denmark presented itself
  As a king of involuntary incandescence.

New York, London, Paris, Rome,
Bless my bed with many a tome.

  Purity of mind is an asphodel
  Strict, fragile, beautiful to tell.
The damage would be to the intellect.

  There would be a cessation of interest,
    Perhaps even a loss of intent
                   if the fig
Of the imagination
            were not left always
Not to pluck.
              She should have flowers
And know the often hours of scintillance,
  But she should fade away if touched.

  Such is the huge disdain
            and the lordly claim
  Of aesthetic dedication;
           such is denial,
  And such is aspiration,
         when fogs of the prince,

Toils of delicate supervision intervene
Between the real
         and the wealth of what seems,
And the mood and the moment is the matter.

The Whole View

I

He has gone into oblivion, who reigned for shading years.
The notion of oblivion interests me. Comfort-kind.

  When children are at the raging point,
  When nerves are at the breaking point,

  When the world shakes an asylum of affront,
  Inhabitable best by strenuous minds in lust,

It is most pleasant to think of dry oblivion,
Think of a man without responsibility.

II

Or of the middle years when, graced by power,
Before the falling off, in the extravagant, able hour

  He felt the worldly play, the gaudy game,
  And tempted home the giant dualisms,

  At ease among destructive speculations,
  Hurling his defiant Ayes, his furious Yeas,

It is agreeable to consider this time well,
The man compact and the world unbreakable.

III

And of youth that wanted to win the chair,
The dare-all glance and the be-all will

  In its swift realizations, swift changes,
  Dauntless courage, despair as deep as death,

33

In the muscular glut, the mind's easy breath,
And running trips where the metaphysical ranges,

It was in that time for a life-time secretly came
Belief in the positive, subsumption of the sublime.

IV

Now to see it all together in one look,
The old, the going, and the young, one bound book

Held in one hand of the God of the Universe,
While other kingdoms and worlds He reads in verse

Of stones, ferns, and stars, discreet enlightenment
Blooming along the place, all used, nothing spent,

Man and nature single and whole in one clarity
Of real myth, in the hold of some divine charity.

Ben Franklin

Sitting in the kitchen
By the Franklin stove,
Ben, your open heater
Is our lightning rod,

Here reality stands off
Sub-zero winter,
(If the furnace failed
We would not philosophize)

Here strikes into us
Reality, as we ask why life
Invokes death,
Why death offers life,

But not to me. Ben the practical,
You do not answer
The deepest questions, nor mine.
Your Americanism

Is not spiritual, thus you
Are limited to inventions
Which please the quotidian
But reject the soul.

But, Ben, is there a soul?
I too am American
And ask you the question.
You are not around to answer.

I say you lack spirit.
You lack the indefinable thrust
To something beyond us,
Which is where I began thinking

And where America has its being.
It is nothing if not aspiring,
And may be nothing again
If it lacks inspiration.

When I think of materialism
I think of death
And when I think of spirit
I think of life.

The spirit must descend
And possess materialists,
Invite them to ascend
Nearer to spirituality

For then can love
Reverse hate,
Man love his fellow
In a social state,

Regenerate.

Lorca

Soon it must come, the great charge,
The caparisonning of belief
And I will step to fight the bull
    A las cinco de la tarde
At five in the afternoon.

I will pass by his horn,
I will be brave and discreet,
The bull of time comes on
    A las cinco de la tarde
At five in the afternoon.

And I will daunt the beast
Near, near to my breast
In the heat of stealthy movement
    A las cinco de la tarde
At five in the afternoon.

And I will taste his breath
In the effort of the real
Whether of life or death
    A las cinco de la tarde
At five in the afternoon.

I will to meet my fate
In the quick play of the steel
    A las cinco de la tarde
In the strength of lust
At five in the afternoon.

A Line of Verse of Yeats

World-famous golden-thighed Pythagoras.
You can take apart the syllables but miss the thigh,
World-famous golden-thighed Pythagoras.
You magically incline into the line of music,
I say this line over, sometimes once a decade,
Or at any odd time of any unspecial year,
The marvel of it, the image without a totality,
No picture of the whole man, what he was doing,
No intellectual picture of a leader, or of a nation,
No rushing to a dictionary of Greek philosophy,
A transfixing experience, sitting in the dark in bed,
Or beside the bed at dawn in a dawn litany,
The magical, lulling line become a lullaby,
I heard it fifty years ago, I hear it now,
World-famous golden-thighed Pythagoras.

Edgar Lee Masters

I am old, stony-faced, and hard,
But I had fire when I was young.

I began telling it like it was
Shortly after it was like it was.

It has never been so again
And I have never been so either.

I felt the real itch of the people
From swinging on their grave stones.

Now I have been made into a stamp.
I always knew I would take a licking.

A Whack at Empson

"Just a Smack at Auden"—*Empson*

Bill, we are hitting seventy.
I remember the startling youngster
Batting ambiguities, your total intelligence
And vivid undergraduate stances.

You made strutting, peacock pronouncements.
It was so heady
Who cared if it was heartless?

You wrote steel-plated poems at twenty,
You were an original of the tight line.
You had life tied in a neat bundle,
No vagabond bag of sticks and tricks,
Wired to science, accommodating astronomy,
You were a computer of necessity.

You took words to such refinement
They might have been refined away
But for their explosive integrity,
Growing to world-clouds today.

But people were growing,
Were living and dying
Calling and crying
For a mastery of suffering,

They were suffering the flesh
In torments of spirit
And you said nothing to them,
Locked in early literary perfection,

Locked in the early line,
The fine strictures of intellectuality,
You had no heart, no blood,
No sex, no guts, no lust in letters

To grapple with older realities.
The people were suffering
Trying, living and dying,
But you were not caring.

I was amazed-dismayed,
You allowed
One new line in your *Collected Poems*,
One line to say in your thirties.
While people were living and dying,
In the universal suffering
Crying for assessment of meaning,
A mastery to live by,
You said nothing.

The forties, the fifties, the sixties,
Yours and the century's, pass.
You won at the start of the race,
Made immortal lines at twenty.

Let others suffer, others struggle,
The whole of life go by.
You said, "It is the pain, it is the pain, endures."
You said, "The waste remains, the waste remains and kills."

These dry, bright, crackling tones
Make you live, although your poetry died.

Eagles

To Allen Tate

Eagles, symbols of our state, lordly birds
Whose wide wings expertly feather air,
Depleted by chemicals we supplied,
Are intractable to write about.

Who would be an eagle? Imperious mien,
Have you seen them traversing the skies?
Majestic sight! Have you seen their talons,
Powerful to subdue enemies?

Hard to adjust to the idea of an eagle!
We fly eagles above our flag.
We have banished them to Alaska. Our division
Is so deep we dare not look at them.
The high! The American ideal! The eagles!

Their eyes, agile, are lofty, specific.
They see more than we, overseers of
Fierce direct gaze beyond duality.
They live beyond the reach of intellect.

This magnificent bird addresses me
With his spirit liable to death.
As the ocean surveillance of the poetic,
If an eagle spirit dies, poetry dies.
If an eagle spirit lives, man flies.

Invective with Suggestions

Hard-headed cranial materialists,
I praise your excellence as mechanics,
You believe in this world, none other,
Your physics never heard of metaphysics.

Bards of the bank books, insured
Against everything but pride and arrogance,
You are the fathers of countless progeny
Begotten in the belief your height is might.

Cold Aristotelians, avid measurers,
Who think that reason can rule the world,
Energetic individualists who deny
Ideas of Plato as beyond you,

Muted advertising muscle-spenders,
Who esteem gross national falsity,
Gut students of your own profit,
Selfish prophets of your own selfishness,

Lords of pride and champions of egotism,
Brave defenders of military strength and killing,
Believers in nationalism over internationalism,
Haters of a world brotherhood of men,

Human beings of untreated error,
I speak for the soul, which does not exist for you,
Soon death will take you away
While the soul will go on living.

The soul has a prescient estate,
It is beyond the small times of extended men
And women, it is final and absolute,
If you do not believe in it it does not care,

If you believe in it it is indifferent,
Which is to say that it has emphatic purity.
Those who do not feel this play foolery.
They think that they have control of time,

The mind is not all, nor are the senses,
The soul provokes thought for millennia,
Evocative, obscure, tantalizing, exquisite,
The soul intrigues and wants us to say yes.

Its defense is something beyond us
Yet in us, the better part of our beings,
Grandiose equipment of heavenly abstraction,
Taste of the heart, sexual thrust and throe,

Capable of discussion, amorphous but real,
Escaping to Jupiter, or beyond the breast,
Soul says forever, but the mind says no.
It is immortal soul, now is our soul.

I aspire to a world soul of nations
Encased in a brotherhood of living beings,
Elect it to totality of consciousness
Whether it exists or not, mankind's grand idea.

The Place

Eventually one finds
There is no environment
Patent for the poetic.

Any place will do.
Alas! One thought of a gold
Hullabaloo, a place of glass

Refinement with subtleties
Crossing the transparency
As lively as mind's images.

One thought of a vast portico
With appropriate, energized
Gods and beings, rich purposes.

Alas! Any place will do.
There is no poetical place,
America continues its practices.

Final toughness of the word,
The word bawling imperfections,
Its paradox to be heard.

II

There used to be
The violent struggle
For place, the right

Place poetic in countries
Or cities or underground,
The right place

Was thought emergent
And to harbor you,
Hello! Poetry Place.

The subconscious was
Nearest, perhaps dearest,
Anyway sheerest

But always fleering off.
Ways you went! Allurement
In echoic happiness.

There was no place for poetry.
Entrenched, my flesh is
Poetry's environment.

Old Dichotomy: Choosing Sides

Why don't you like the wild cry of the madman.
Who does not know what makes him cry as he does?

Because Aristotle said the world was measurable,
Took leaves off every tree, and measured them.

He began the scientific method. But the wild man
Was perhaps older, subjective, would scoff at the objective.

We have to choose between the wild in us, and the sober,
The intensity of genius may be the best,

In it we recognize some true likeness,
Strugglers for change, visionaries of a bright future,

Keenest sensibilities eager for anything new,
Knowers of the first source of universal acclaim,

Shelley, Blake, and Lawrence knew of this essence
Of mighty realities thrown off as felt abstractions,

And why does the world have to be so slow and practical
As not to live for high vision instead of scientific clay?

And why was Plato deeper by far than Aristotle,
The far light he saw of absolutes, the Eternal Types,

Allied him with creativity at the heat of creation,
Even the new physics represented a principle of indeterminacy.

And why do we cherish the mad poets rather than the sane
If we do not feel the truth of the immeasurable?

The truth of the incalculable, wild imagination
Where anything goes, and nothing is held back,

The genius of total illimitable, essential man
Who knows the joy of what it is to be free.

⋅⋖ T W O ⋗⋅

Two Translations from
Justice without Revenge (*El Castigo sin Venganza*),
by Lope de Vega (1562–1635)

*(Adapted to English rhymed couplets from the prose translation of
Jill Booty)*

DUKE:

Do you not know, Ricardo, that a play
Mirrors yesterday, as it mirrors today
The foolish and the wise, the young and the old,
Courtier, Governor, King, Warrior, Maiden, Wife, all told,
They may learn from plays, they may ponder
In this quick mirror the shifts of life and honor.
Our customs show forth both the fickle and severe.
Truth and mockery mingle together here.
The true entertainer is the censurer
Who brings both wit and tragedy to bear.
I have heard enough already of my reputation.
Do you wish to feed me now another ration?
Recall, the Dukes are hedged about,
Not used to hearing truth told out.

BATIN:

Your Father, after living very libidinously
And being criticized for this, even piteously
By his family and friends, has come
To wish to live in virtue and in quiet,
In fact, to have virtue as his only diet.
There is no diet more memorable
Than marriage to keep a man honorable.
Once a vassal and servant of great France's king
Gave him a remarkable and beautiful thing,
A horse named Swan, with the swanlike glow
Of a beautiful animal as white as snow.

This play, in the author's adaptation, was produced in its entirety under the
title *The Bride from Mantua* at the Hopkins Center, Dartmouth College, May
5–9, 1964.

51

His head was proud. When he tossed his mane
Waves and ripples like a sea came
From his ears even down to his restive feet.
This fine beast had the high pride and fleet
Disdain that the most beautiful women possess
To let not the most skillful trainer caress them.
The king, noticing this marked beauty and ill use
Thought to change the situation by abuse.
He ordered Swan put into a pit
With a fierce lion already in it.
When the nervous creature saw the lion there
He bristled all over his body every hair
And his mane, no longer smoothly flowing
Stood like lances packed together, going
Down his head and neck. The proud horse was meek
As a hedgehog that shivers and sweats a speck
Of gall from every hair.   A dwarf sat on his back.
Swan, so meek now that he would not fight back,
His spirit quelled by any potential lion attack,
Would let even a child ride on his back.

Protection

Opening a drawer
After winter, up stairs,
I found a field mouse
In a nest
With inch-long babies.

Not to disturb them
I descended,
Sat in a chair
Contemplating
Fragility,

Astounded in silence.
The mother field mouse
Fell down steps
Clutching an infant
In her mouth.

Cautiously moving to the kitchen
She deposited her kind
In a new place
Underneath
The kitchen sink.

How could she
Leap up the stairs,
Fall down each step
Many times,
Bringing no harm?

I long sitting
Watched the still drama.
O white-footed mouse,
Small mother,
How I praised you.

Mother Swallow

The swallow mother is kept incredibly busy
To feed her birdlets
By catching bugs on the wing.

At full tide before set of sun
It is a pleasure to sit still
Looking at the water,

Looking at the sky and pines,
And then to see
Mother swallow swoop

Or even go straight along
And swoop up a bug.
Bee-line it to the nest

And feed the bugs to the little ones,
One little one at a time,
Which requires more flight and bugs.

While I feel free
Taking my ease,
The swallow is busy by necessity.

We are both held in nature.
I admire her wings,
She cannot admire my pen.

Life is incontestable.
Death is immeasurable,
But why talk about it?

Those who are cruising on the deep
Will pull down their sails now
Awaiting July's hottest moonlight night.

Everybody is lined up for love.

Fear Death by Water

I like to see the bay filled up with boats,
Which argues interest and continuity,
Argues that man controls the ocean,
Which he does not, but seems to do,

None of these vessels has been sunk or damaged
And short of a hurricane will not be this month,
The pleasure mankind takes in defying the seas
Grips him as he raises a sail, or increases a throttle,

He will defy the ocean waters, take a reef
If necessary, love life from a flying deck,
Yet yesterday a man drowned in Buck's Harbor,
Drunk, capsized, took salt water in his lungs.

Poems will not save him. I am afraid of the sea,
But he was not, was not, so he is nought.

Better Management

Science stood in the eye of the light
And spoke like an oracle of fate:
    I am the discoverer, I discover
    That I am the destroyer of the world.

I can rock the oceans, rock the seas,
My bomb will atomize the earth.
    I can blow mankind away,
    There will not be another day.

Art came forth into the sunlight
And blessed the land and the heart of man:
    I redeem man from destructive knowledge,
    I am the way to joy and love.

I am a mystery of revelation.
I am the hand that gives, not takes away.
    Harmonious, not explosive,
    A silent spirit, whole and clean.

Storm and Quiet

The difference between reacting to a storm,
Whose eye is malevolent, and whose violence
Kills hundreds of people, knocks properties apart,

And reacting to a poem, whose violence
Is of a different caliber and may disturb
A reader sitting in an armchair contemplating

Ancient mysteries of Chinese dynasties,
Infinite subtleties of Indian mythologies,
Is a question of thinking and of being.

If you are being yourself and a storm comes,
The violent force of nature, you have to move
To put your vessel up in a safe harbor,

To take steps not to be destroyed by nature.
But if it is not a question of survival,
Of the vessel or of yourself, and you are allowed

To think, that is a delectable proposition.
You are allowed to think while the storm passes,
Chance has opened your mind to possibilities

And you say, I have survived the hurricane nature
And I am allowed to think of the meaning of things.
You think of the meanings with gratitude,

But you do not tell your fellows what they are.
For what if you had told them everything,
You would have named the monster destroying the vessel

And you.

Hysteria of Communication

There is hysteria of communication.
Hostages are held in a far country.
What should we do?

Communications are bumped off satellites.
We have polluted space with particles.
We are not too particular what we do.

Can art cope with this? Both sides
Are right and wrong, are wrong and right.
Evil, distributed by gaming table whirl.

Would killing do any good? Man the killer
Is equal to killing any man any time.
Killing resolves but does not solve.

There are poets in Arabia who are serene,
Beyond the hysteria of communication.
They write of love, in a pleasing innocence.

These young poets face bloody revolution.
They prefer to think in terms of millennia.
                              What should they do?

Transformation

The lilac speaks without a voice: pure blue.
Weather has not killed it,
Nor storms riven it,
The sky has descended and kissed it into you.

You are the lilac hanging in the air.
You are blue speechless beautiful being, all fair
And graceful in escapelessness,
All lilac, blue-found beyond evasiveness.

Opposition

Wildness of nature is in Florida,
Where senses open to the enveloping heat,
Where no Puritan lives, persons respond to excess,
The lust of the idea of Paradise.
Where Ichetucknee springs from limestone depths
Changeless through clear centuries,
As we float tubing down the enchanting stream.

Tameness of nature holds back the North,
Desolations of the past eroding the present,
The long, heavy shadow of the Puritans
Teaches the severe. They thought life could be better,
Prayed to God not to do anything wrong,
Held back their passion, aimed to kill,
Burned as witches free life-loving girls.

Incidence of Flight

I spring joy out of my rib cage
Like a flash of pigeons flying North
South here in Mississippi, Florida,

I insist on the aspiring eye,
Try as time does to cast it down,
Cast up the eye, birds their blue nature

Transfer through the air from the soul
Whole in its ambiguous essence
From one place to another

Without waste, we follow them
Ten times higher for their flight
Because we dream the same dream

Teeming in space out of our rib cage,
Age shall not deter us, nor walking stale
Flying, we are going up high in joy

On blue air, as if birds were the spirit,
Man was meant to walk, but meant to fly
Joyful as pigeons full of the grace of space

And if we have joy we have love
Above all else. Flare up, love in the heart
Part of flying, spring joy in Mississippi, in Florida,

It is a tale bold as an ideogram,
Conclamant wings heading North
Forth away. Joy uncages man to love.

The Swinging Bridge

When an hour is harmonious
    Destruction lurks
    Inside the ear.

When you think of good life
    Inside your body
    A wild cell.

When in strength of love
    Imagine the weakness
    To come on you.

What of a thousand years?
    You cannot tout
    The meaning.

Lover to lover, eye to eye,
    Destruction lives, also,
    Inside the eye.

Walk across a swinging bridge,
    Make love in the afternoon.
    That's it. And fit.

Mistaken Identity

The man who ate mushrooms
And tried to crucify himself
Cutting a stake, piercing hands,
Then feet, then hanging on vines,
Then walking home and stabbing himself
With a two-inch knife didn't make it.

If he got higher he had sunk lower
But instead of giving was only getting
When in confusion he presented
Himself to himself as J. Christ
It was pathetic. So mushroom busted
The bastard blamed the world on his ills.

If he had given himself to others
Instead of giving himself to himself,
Blasted on the heath of misadventures,
He might have reset the delicate
Balance of nature unbalanced by tricky
Gestures, he might have vomited mushrooms,

But, prized by the spirit of overkill,
It almost got him over underkill
Whereupon he had proved that hell
Is the joke of time, and been no man.
He is walking around sewed up,
A man beginning all over again.

The Great Trees

The great trees are at ninety degrees,
Hot wind blowing them back and forth
As twilight develops. High in a condominium

I watch them practically at their tops.
They wonder why they have to sway, but they sway
Beautifully, a forest of eventuations.

The wind is their master, sways them, it is
Persuasion. You think they accept stillness or wind.
What else can they do? They are like the human race.

If I were a tall tree I would like to be
My own being, and not be swayed by a wind.
I would like to breathe in my own nature

And give out my own nature for anybody to see.
If a bird lit on my limb I would let him sing,
If a man brought an ax to my base I would hate him.

The great trees are hot, they experience Florida.
Stillness is no more remarkable than a high wind.
Swaying trees do not know the nature of poetry.

I am enamored of their extreme sensuosity.
They are as sensual as supposedly intellectual flesh.
They express an incredible kind of whelming richness,

I try to feel into their very beings, being
Foreign man to the world of ecstatic vegetation,
The great trees are steadfast in their lovingness.

Ichetucknee

It is the continuous welling up from the earth
We must remember. Dawn comes, and the waters
Spring fresh, clear, vital from the earth.
Night comes, they well unabated from the dark.

Strange, is it not, that the temperature
Is always the same. The clarity is without change.
As the water blooms upward to become a petaled river
Each grain of sand below is visible as in air.

Over the oval, the mouth, the maw, the source,
We cannot see down into the cavernous mystery
Into primitive limestone releasing the clear water.
We are impelled outward from the warm, strong center.

Our bodies delight in the flow of original life.

Freely in the stream of exhilarating non history
We can walk, swim, float in the clearest shallows.
Upon us the welling up of the source,
Around us the gift of the river, the way we must go.

Our bodies delight in the flow of original life.

News of the World

Design Research is going out of business.
A news flash. It was the new Harvard,
A name that gave new life to a quarter of a century.
Perhaps they did not research design enough.
All such news gives me a time pain,
It is the passing of the world none can help.

Before Design Research Wallace Stevens
Walked down Hilliard Street and told us
Of an old friend at Hilliard Street and Brattle,
A lady who read at the Shakespeare Society.
The building was torn down even in his time.
Change is the steps of changelessness.

What is the design of the universe,
And what shall we do for its research?

Harvard Stadium

Sitting at the top of the stadium
The poet who was beyond this age, felt
Superior to the football players down below
Struggling back and forth on the turf.

He felt the elan of the senses, young muscles
Exhibiting prowess on the field of youth.
They were captive in their presences,
Held in bondage by youth's inferiority.

So felt the sage, his fame secure in age
While these youth could not foresee the future.
Some would win, some lose, in worldly struggles.
He was indifferent to victory or defeat.

Life was a struggle. He was known in the world
As one who had won the prize of worldly acclaim.
He sat above the battle like a god,
With lordly eye viewing the happenings.

No matter, now, who won or lost,
His musings unnoticed by the spectators.
He was a quiet victor at the spectacle,
The reddest judge of the rueful scene.

So God himself might sit apart, and stare
At the antics of the animal man,
Seen from above millennia of wars and non-war,
Indifferent to the players down below.

The Airy Vent

It was an airy vent
Went up the sky
And was my love,
Up high.

Don't know where it went,
Don't know what it was
But an airy vent
Overcame opposition.

Opposers live in a real world
Of what the world praises,
The here and now,
But the airy vent amazes.

I live for extravagances
By them I know
The truth of the real,
The green flash.

Dark Memories

Dark memories are more persistent
Than light memories of incontestable joy

When flags are flying, and wild white wind
Blows the elegant birds about the sky,

And the throat catches unable to speak
For the majesty, the danger and ecstasy of nature,

O the great moments of instantaneous recognition
When you are lost in a world beyond the human,

Yet a part of it, being one with nature
When you become the gull, the eagle, the osprey,

A feeling so ancient as to be so tenuous
That you arrive at an existence before words,

You are life-force and enigma, you are true
Because it is before any cause of failure

And you are a part of the spirit of the universe
Before intellect forced you into human particularity,

What a joyful moment before birth, beyond death,
This oneness, a gift, a glimpse, a glory,

When everything lives in creativity, you are
Gulls' wings, eagle's eye, the lightning's flash,

You are all brightness, haleness, ununderstandable joy
Before dark memories occlude the bright reaches.

Feat

To say it out—to say it all—to peak
Before falling over the cliff—El Capitan—
Molecules bundling—The togetherness—
Then the shattering fall—

Or better to have no dashes, Emily,
Better to be subtle and discreet,
As subtle as the writher in the grass,
Whose measures not taken, who missed your feet.

Gainsville Sun

Sun, you are going down, you have got me down,
There is no use to compete with you, you win.
A few decades against millions of years.

You haven't told me why I am sentient,
Or why you began, in an inhuman way,
In a cubicle of chemicals. No discourse.

You are a disc, of course. That is my joke, not yours.
Is it not queer that you are the giver of heat
And light, but I cannot turn you on or off?

No, you would say, if you had our gift of speech,
Your arrogance is preposterous, you are of small matter,
I am an energy field of galactic asseverations

Imperfectly chemical, astronomical, sidereal, nonpoetical,
You do not have to bring your problems to me, I am
Killer sun, sooner or later, but smile upon you now,

A speck in the universe, and what should I care about
Oddities, vagaries, absurdities of the human race
Doomed to mentality and death, while I am vicious viscous

Reality? If you had perception you would use my heart,
It would preserve you on the planet, not deplete me.
Whether you do this I swear I do not care.

I beam. Eye, beam.

Words

Words, because the sun is going down.
Words, to believe words are imperishable.

Words, to memorize ancient words.
Catullus wanted to be read in 2000 A.D.

Words, who is the greatest comedian?
He points fun at our gaitless longings.

Words, will they be displaced by
Electric gainsayings, mock Blake and Hopkins?

Words, most of us know only one language.
Consider multiple languages, the one

Language of God. Why think of it? It brings pain.
Medics say that pain is a sign of life.

The dead are painless. The more pain you
Can stand, the better. Poetry, pain and pleasure.

Words, exquisite integers. A word
Is as beautiful as the face of a child

Before he or she can speak a word.
Words, integers of possibility.

The word of God, the word of a lover, word
Of blasphemers who hated life

Because they loved it so much, primal energy,
The words of Satan are sweet to some.

Word, if you cannot speak a word what do you know?
The mute who cannot speak a word

May know more than authors of sixteenth-century poems.
The mute must be equated with the articulate

After death has removed both from
The field of life. Upsprung words.

Who could not love word-music of Beethoven,
Of Mozart, the sounds of Wordsworth,

And of Blake, of others you may love,
If we could have heard them voice their poems.

Resonant possibility unrealized.
Yet many heard Dylan Thomas

Whose voice was angel order
In some heaven believed in before he was born.

He expressed a magical reality of poetry.
Words, the word of God, what is the word of God

But the word of man?

The Words

The words—
                    I deny you to myself because I
Hold all the secrets. You intrude upon me
Every time you write. I want to be secret.
I want to defy you because you are insistent.

You want to find out the secret of poetry.
I want to keep you from finding out the secret.
If you destroyed me you might become immortal
Writing a poem that might be read in short future,

Like Marvell, or in long future, like Dante.
Nobody can imagine more than a few thousand years.
I do not want you to capture me even for ten years.
I am the substratum of the Bible, or every great work,

I do not want you to get any new ideas out of me.
I am words. I am the words of truth and of reality.
If any poet reaches my secret, and writes a poem
Rich, truthful enough to last a hundred years

I should feel chagrin, because I feel intact
And if any poet assails and conquers my mastery,
I want to be mastered, but I want to remain virgin.

This is the dramatic situation of the centuries,
That poets want words to conquer time.
To be immortal, but that words withhold their wish,
And veil themselves in immortal unconquerability.

Specifications

Where is the word that will last?
Is it the last word or the first?

Is it the word you cannot say?
Ancients said you cannot say God.

Is it the inarticulate word
Said into the ear of a lover?

Is it Wallace Stevens' conviction
Nothing good but a physical world?

Stone-faced Emerson professing
Transcendentalism is "a little beyond"?

Is it the expansions of Whitman,
Or the contractions of Dickinson?

Is it Frost afraid of Jesus
Or Jeffers afraid of man?

Is it providential Auden
Who only believed here and now?

Is it the suicides who said nothing
But the speech of their own suicides?

Is it the memory of Plato
Which lasts as long as poetry?

The word I am thinking of,
Which will last, is love.

Accuse it, abuse it, you will
See that it will not kill.

Reading an Old Poem

It is not right. It did not
Get the words right. Who could write
A poem with all words right
That would always be right on?

It was three centuries ago
When the poet said, I
Will write what is right,
Write the truth right now.

If it was the truth,
And he was a right word-wright
Who would write right then
The news, why is it false now?

Some words right themselves
After period-falls, stand straighter
Later on, make us elate
For a poem's lovely sake.

Why some fall, some rise, some stay
Has to do with
Genius of language it is called,
And that is a mystery.

The Poem

The poem is like the body,
If it is heavy, it should be heavy;
If light, be light. If indifferent,
Indifferent to heaviness or lightness,
Ordinary as ordinary mankind.
Many poems are this ordinary.
If fanatical, fanatical; if Gothic,
Embellished; if prosaic, then prosaic.

Speculation is more of the poem
Than of the bodies that make the poems.
It tends to be so. The analogy is imperfect.
So is the body, yet we esteem poems
Of contrived perfection, intricacies
Of imagination, cunning, sinuous,
Impetuous yet controlled; the air fighter
Knows how to measure the throttle.

The Year

The poetry of the world is like the sun,
To which all aspire in Winter; in Winter
In high Alaska the sun is a little joke,
Peeping up, and then going under.
The Eskimos are left pretty much in the dark.

The sun on the equator, however, is high,
The heat excessive, people take light for granted.
Equatorialists believe perforce in an open poetry
While arctic folk believe in a closed poetry—
They are more suicidal than equatorialists.

What happens in between, where most of us live?
If the poetry of the world is like the sun,
In the current millennium the sun is kindly.
We are neither frozen nor scorched to death
But live in the changes of four seasons.

There is the Winter, when the bears hibernate,
And groundhogs, they give up, peacefully sleep.
And every man and woman in New Hampshire or Vermont
Feels the challenge of the cold, and goes about
Feeling triumph to survive the Winter.

Then comes Spring, and the mud season, alternate
Cold and warmth, a long time coming.
It holds itself back, half dead, but gradually
Signifies an amazing, new enlargement
And soon there are buds on the pussy willows.

Then there is Summer, like a great clarion call.
The sun has climbed up to the top of the mountains.
The young and the old, those in between,
Take splendor, magnitude, and heat for granted,
It is the greatest time of life for people.

In grand summer people live poetry without writing it.
Autumn brings on the poetry of melancholy,
It always has, and it probably always will.
If you are melancholy it is because time passes.
You wonder what is the meaning of the world.

Thinking: Being

I can't imagine silence more silent
Than thought: thought is a night of day.
Thought is so deep, replete, and dark
That it is our most brilliant part.

Thought is the day-cling of our being.
It is the unsilence of what we have to say,
It is the evocation of the unsayable:
The mystery of the imagination: a way

Of being, the heart of care, hope, despair,
So still you can hear yourself being still,
Time and space made one, past and future
Existing in immediacy beyond the will.

Delicious stillness! Unthought of thought.
If you thought of it you hadn't ought to.

Lying Still

And all that mighty heart is lying still.
It is telling lies all the time. I thought silence
Was intended, carried by the felt emotion.
I never thought Wordsworth was Machiavelli

Yet Shakespeare studied hypocrisy in the heart of London,
All that mighty heart was the Macbeths and Iago,
Coriolanus, therefore why should supreme silence
Be anything to talk about, when rife, red hypocrisy

Is more interesting and central to the heart of man?
Lovers are lying still, in the stillness of spent passion?
Lovers are still telling lies to each other night long,
They are living in fantasy, and will not give it up.

I am lying still to tickle this conundrum,
If I told the truth of the lie, it would be lying still.

John Finley

I

While three hundred Americans died in flight
From a broken nut, in cracked materialism,
Here on the stage a man appeared so fine
That he became the essence of immateriality.

He became iridescent in limitless belief,
His entire life became his luminous speech,
His face beamed that of the gods he loved,
His voice almost supernatural in its reach,

Yet human, the mingling of reality and unreality,
The vision, the passionate control of the ancient Greeks.
He became, in his astonished, firing mind

Plato and Socrates, he seized Sophocles,
There shone Odysseus the sufferer, Penelope alone,
And claimed the great Achilles for his own.

One man to speak beyond three hundred
Who died of a broken nut in a fiery crash
Of materialism, matter splattered on the earth,
One man, incandescent, to preserve our heritage

Of the greatness of the human past
When gods and men lived closely together,
When death was not meaningless, and harmony
Prevailed as love and wonder in all weather.

One man so rational and so keen
That he was transformed before our transfixed eyes
And became the gods that we had seen
When we were young to wildness, to wild cries.

He was a man radiant as history, as we
Stood to the glory of an ancient story.

Emerson's Concord

Dear Ralph, to your Great Stone Face,
I would not have called you Ralph in your time,
The intimacy draws me closer to you,
You were here in Concord, your young wife had died,

Or was it the other Concord, this excites me
That we have two Concords. I do not know which one
Where your spirit hovers over the late fall landscape
And if it were the other one, the distance is not great.
Dualism as opposites has kept me from unison,
Unitarian simplicity ignores the grapes of wrath.

In my operant dualism I do not have to be Emersonian
Exclusively. I can also be Whitmanian,
And to break the mold in favor of no limits to poetry,
I can be Trinitarian, call Emily Dickinson Mary.

Dear Ralph, if you were an old poet at this banquet,
What would you make of our upheaved century?
You ventured as far west as Chicago, then daring to do,
To back American business, believe in our expansion,

But what today would you say of World War II, Korea,
Vietnam, bombing Cambodia, fascist Watergate,
Our fear of law, our fear of impeachment,
What would you think of millennial radioactivity?

You had the word as in your time, Ralph, complexity
Of language made simple for all to hear, you teach
To sense the supernatural in the natural,
Wit remarking that Transcendentalism is a little beyond.

This poem was first read at a dinner in Concord, N.H., honoring the author's appointment as Poet Laureate of New Hampshire in 1979.

Poetry and Games

I

The lightweight poets are happier,
They wave a silken handkerchief,
A necklace,
Toss up baubles here and there.

However, the heavyweight poets
Kick you in the groin
Disobeying the rules,
Wrestle you to the floor

Like the Golden Greek.
When they have got you down
They kick you in the groin.

They jump up and down on you.
Didn't you know
You should have been savaged before?
They say

There is no tragedy in tragedy
No fun
But smashing idols,
Truth is the work of fools.

II

However, the middleweight poets
Would like to smash you
But do not have the weight,
The gall,

They play it both ways,
Tinsel here, cynicism there,
It is all a game,
A world to make,

A laugh, a tent stake.
They play it straight,
A feint, a biff, no Frank Gotch.

They're skating out
Northeast
Southwest
West, east, south, north

Somebody is hurt, puck in the face,
He's in the box, no, he's out,
They're skating out, blue line
Timing, win, lose.

Maine Summer High Color Luncheon

Sufficiently high over Muscongus Bay
Looking afar to islands, open ocean subverted,
Blues, whites, greens dazzling the eyesight, and
Flowers telling their truth, elders
Gather on the lawn in high, dry, clean, light air,
Matisse-striped, before a table of drinks
Of reflective colors, radishes, carrots, cauliflowers,
Onions, vegetable efflorations, lobster sandwiches,

Persons survivors of shredded decades,
Philanthropist, governor, teacher, painter,
Looking complex, one cancer-abated,
Coming to the highland island by outboard power
Agilely evading lobster pots, persons bright characters
Streaked in knowledge of separation, marriage, divorce,
Children, grandchildren, flecked by gauzy light,
Hummingbirds thought red sugar-water flasks real flowers.

The Truth

The only hope is to catch the moment as it flies.
We lift our spirits to this hope and salute the wind.
The wind is the reservoir of being. All go
Into the play of time on our flesh and bones.

We think to hold our loves and hopes intact
Yet when we love, love flies away from us.
When we feel that we have harmony and control
Cancer rips the life out of our lungs, or bowels.

Grace and charm, finitely flexible,
Make the old Viennese dance with joy as they
Sway to the music, revealing rhythms that
Capture spirit in delicate order and ardor.

Men and women know the fear of death,
When all shall be taken away from us, yet the
Inexpressible approached in poetry,
Careen of man in keens of music.

The wind of the spirit blows over mankind.
It is the vast gesture of the universe.
To have felt the pulse of deepest being
Is to catch eternity in the moment, life in death.

And the young shall try it again, the old
Regret they cannot express the inexpressible.
Fervor, effort, the dance, wild spirit
Flow and stay in the mind, and the soul

Shall worry the flesh to come up to it
And the flesh in ecstasy will deny the soul,
The flesh afraid of so great a prospect,
The flesh knows it will die torn apart.

As the music sways us in strife and charm
The only hope is to catch the moment as it flies.
It flies from us. We cannot know
The ultimate purpose of either life or death.

Pick up the guitar, swing your girl, love the real,
It is all illusion that you think you know.
Necessity will take and shake you by the backbone,
The end for the living is a place too slow.

What hope, then? Catch your spirit out of the air,
Rejoice in resiliency of being, and being free
Sing the song of the song of splendors, sing,
See the light, sing, stop, sing, see the light.

Address to Time

Poet

Why am I going away to the elders?
Why cannot I stay with the young?

Time

The young do not know where they are.
You know, but you do not master me.

Poet

I reject the human condition.

Time

When I win you worry no more.

Poet

I see the wrecks you have made of men,
Stroke victims, half paralyzed, in hospital.

Time

You cannot escape, I will get you.

Poet

I defy you with the word outlasting you.

Time

The joke is on you but not on me.
You see, I have been present for ages.

Poet

You may destroy my body but not my mind.
My poetry will outlive your insults.
I have a vision of eternity.

Time

Go as far as you like. Think anything.
Feel anything. Write anything.

Dante lived a thousand years ago
But I defeat him, he will not live forever.

Poet

I speak the reality of my being,
I have the power to deny your name.
I consider that my words are timeless.

Time

When you saw the decrepit bodies
In the hospital, victims of strokes,
You must have recognized my inviolability.

Poet

I have a secret weapon, the soul.
You may think the soul is invisible,
You may think it does not exist,
But my soul defies you, invincible.

Time

This is a child's idea of reality.
There is no soul, and my servant death
Will divest you of any of it you thought you had.

Poet

What are you? When I look into the garden,
See the sumptuous lilacs, the yellow day lilies,
When I behold the breast or the eye,
I know that I serve the sensuous world,
That you serve me, I do not fear you.

Time

Love as you will to the depth of humanity,
The fact is that my impersonality
Lives to destroy your personality.

And that whatever delights you find in love
I will not permit it to continue,
And I bring to your love death.

Poet

> You say words I do not wish to hear,
> I do not hear them. My passion disrupts you
> And in one moment of union and bliss
> I have overcome your arguments.

Time

> You are my enemy because you can dream
> Of something beyond me. Yet I am true,
> And you are a web of lies and deceits.

Poet

> I feel I am human but you are inhuman.
> I feel that a kiss destroys your argument,
> My psyche dreams beyond your seeming.

Address to God

Thanks, God, for it being not
                         Malignant.
An instant transcontinental
                         connection
Three hours after the operation
Answered that you made it, this time,
                         Benign.

Thanks, God, for it being
                         Not Malignant.

Last week, though, my friend
Received the opposite news from you,
                         Malignant.

I maintained stoical calm both times,
                         Afraid

To let frenzy drive me to some wailing wall.

I throw my force at you in any case,
                         Humiliated

Not to have your power. If I had it
I don't think I would torture
                         the human race.

I do not know what is true,
I am not as malignant as you.

Prayer to the God of Harm, The Song of the Poet

Do not take my suffering away from me,
I recognize paranoia as joy.
I hate suffering, but I enjoy it.
I recognize your strong arm God of Harm.

I am put down into a position of pain.
It is a great pain without a cure.
But if not pain, I would have pride,
In pride's folly be dissatisfied.

God of Harm do not release me, or help me,
Do not cease from abateless strokes.
It is through suffering that I sing,
Do not let me go, keep me suffering.

❧ T H R E E ☙

Still

Teach us to sit still. Aware of
No motion, peace, being hale. It is
Earthly, not heavenly, we do not
Know of heaven, know of earth rest

When silence and stillness pervade the room,
Occupy us to no occupation.
Delicious! Like the moment of pause
Before eating a cumquat. Cum what?

Why, before life is oppressive again
We sit in ourselves densely repressive,
Able to contemplate flesh as soul,
Employ the illusion of thinking we are whole.

Still, More

At twenty-five I ran up Times Square
To the Park trying to catch myself.
An engine of action, fiercely efficient.
No idea of why I was going so fast.

Fast as frenzies of imagination,
A Pegasus clipping the pavement.
Joy of the world, paragon animal,
No restraint, genius of being.

At seventy-five I derided this,
The world uncatchable by speed.
I sat still, my mind composed,
Knowing orders of infinity.

Still, Further

Thinking is superior to action,
Contemplation an endless inaction

When time seems to stop, lopped
Off things you had to do.

Contemplation, silence, regenerative,
Restore innate balances in the being.
Being alive is being able to dream
Limitless flashes of infinitude.

By stillness we achieve the planet,
By contemplation we surround the stars.
The head is the instrument of knowing,
The heart has necessity of God.

Of Truth

For Robert Penn Warren

We were going to say the truth
But we talked so long that the truth fled.
Where it went we do not know.
    It was believed as some kind of absolute
    As we were more and more resolute.

If it is true that there is no absolute
It is true that everything is relative,
Then this relative becomes a new absolute.
    The resolution is in being able to talk.
    If man fails he is unable to walk.

We think of the truth of Plato, or Aristotle.
We think of the truth of Stratford Shakespeare,
We think of the truth of our father and mother.
    After a while the big principles slipped.
    The *tabula rasa* was not true, but ripped.

The truth lives, despite our lies and evasions.
The truth is beyond the mind to grasp.
Time corrupts the innocence of childhood.
    Time is the jester of the days,
    Truth will evade us all our ways.

Truth despairs of telling the truth, and says
To the mind and soul it is full of lies.
The cave man painted himself out of simplicity.
    The Nobel Prize winner is full of despair
    That truth is not true, despite his care.

He cannot think that he has won truth
Because there is something beyond the absolute,
And that is the absolute of the relative.
    He sees that mankind has given him a prize
    But in the night he says, I am not true, nor wise.

The Invitation of the Evening

There is a cold mist hovering around the evening,
A stasis as boats lie tied up in the harbor.
We have heard of the calm before the storm,
It is so calm as to be somewhat ominous.

The light darkens after the sun has departed,
You wonder what portends. If lightning,
Like yesterday, you hope it won't kill anybody.
The children are playing badminton in semidark.

No good to think of ten thousand years ago.
In those days all the islands were mountain peaks.
Odd to think that I am looking at the same sight
Not seen before man was on this planet.

It is not thought that the ocean is quiet.
It does not look dangerous in the growing evening.
A late gull calls, and a far sea bell.
Pretty soon everybody will be unconscious.

And it didn't matter that the race of man occurred,
Mankind will be sleeping, the ocean will be asleep,
Everything will be a vastness, there will be no poetry,
Silent sea night surrogate for eternity.

News

The news today is not bad.
It is that the sun has arisen.
This is the greatest news of the world.
Our newspapers give much bad news.
The earth is still riding around the sun,
We are earth-riders through galaxies.

The news today is not bad again.
The race of mankind lives today.
Men-women have not blown themselves
Off the earth, or blown the planet apart.
There are men-women of all shapes, temperaments
Who are living this life from life to death.

The news is that the moon still exists.
It is an instance of loving importance
Because brash man has now brushed her surface.
The moon has ceased to be a poetical virgin.
Will she bear good poems present or future?
Poets have yet to write a seminal moon poem.

The news today is good as to God.
Although some think that she/he does not exist
It is hard to beat the argument of Pascal.
He saw a watch in the mud; he deduced
That it had been made by somebody.
He looked at the world, and thought the same.

After God, we can only go to the devil.
The news is that the devil is alive and well.
The devil gets himself most in the news
Because we love him, and he loves us.
If I could say that order outlives chaos
It is because the devil reminds us of hell.

A Certain Distance from Man

An artist should be at a certain distance
From man,
He cannot be at one with him entirely
Or there would
Be no point in being an artist,
Which means
To be set apart to state the general.

If you are a general man
You are immersed in society as it is,
See no reason for stating what it is like,
The day suffices, your life suffices.
The artist is a person set apart
Compelled to evaluate and make manifest
The unrealizable effort in the human condition.

While I am breathing a few breaths
The moon has moved off from the pine tree
Standing over the ocean, moving to the right,
In twilight with murmurations of full tide,
And I can no more stop the moon from
Going right than I can stop this poem.
There is an order in the heavens
And there is an order in the heart of man.
Harmony is so great a wonder
That you wonder at the power of nature
To produce in me a sense of magnitude,
Great quiet, immeasurable wholeness
When sun sets as the moon moves right,
Visibility is allied to vastness,
I capture the spirit of the universe
In time beyond destruction, fantasy, or sea bells.

Youth and Age

I remember when I was little and the world was great
A storm crashed the trees, lightnings vociferated,
Dark horror darkened the house, we descended
To the cellar in cold fear, in stupefying dread,
In wordless terror. I clung to the skirts of my mother.

Now I am old, and life continues, time is small.
Facing whatever may bring the end of the world
I have no better answer, now than then—
Blind clutches against the force of nature,
A wild glimpse, and poetry.

Sunset over Florida

The great sun, sun drastically there, the
What I forget for the word for the sun
Better than Gustave Doré, almost instantaneous
Changes in the big spectacular event of the late
Afternoon changing to evening with spectacular
Cloud formations in pink, red, yellow, gold,
Amethyst, ruby, wind propelling the scene
Making the setting of the sun not-worldly deceptive,
Although this has been going on—but is not
Tonight unique?—millions of years.

The Pan panorama of the sensuous heavens
In Florida, where balmy breezes bring
Multitudinous egrets to rest on Bivens Arm
Across the lake in the trees; where
The wheeling hawks have quieted
From rolling over the trees in search of something;
Where the alligators are out of the picture
Of grackles, cardinals, woodpeckers on high,
They are down below in the murk of downy waters.
The sun descends, put an end to the poem.

But hold. The grasp of the absolute is the
Grasp of the palpable, clear in the eye,
Yet the dusk descending accelerates the impalpable.
The dark, the heavy, the impalpable, we are
Forgiven for the ecstasy of the highest sunset
Verities of even spiritual but real revelations
By the oncoming darkness, quick near the equator,
No twilight, or little, until all of a sudden
The balm of the breeze riffles our soft skin
Until we are surrounded by darkness and deception.

The Impersonal

The impersonal states the case for nature,
Like it or not. It cares not for you or me.
Look, I am looking at the sunset,
(I might as well be looking at the sunrise)
A gorgeous spectacle in the state of Florida
(It could be any state) over Bivens Arm
(It could be a hundred mile desert from Tucson).

Look, I am looking at the sunset
But it could not be said to be looking at me.
(Or the dawn either.) The sun is impersonal,
Does not know whether it is 10,000 B.C.
Or April Fool's Day in 1978.
The sun is inflammatory, inflames me.
I put on a protective coating, Pre-Sun.

I sat in the same place a year ago,
My enthusiasm for nature was joyous,
I looked out and felt well within, without
Giving a thought to the nature of nature.
Here, a year later, I am convinced that nature,
Seen in the sun going down through the trees,
Cares nothing for mankind, nothing for me.

I care for nature and for the sun,
Whether at sunset or at dawn, and I care
To state that I am in a state of joy
In beholding her, however impersonal,
And that I give my personal recognizance
In an accolade of bootless praise,
Though she lives millennia, rejoice in my moment.

Winter

St. Lucy's day
Darkens me
The sun
Sub zero

How to rejoice
In the dead of winter
With no choice,
Wool-blanketed.

Give in
To this death,
Ultimately we
Have no breath.

Learn to
Be nothing,
Hopeless,
Not to sing.

Learn to be free
In nothingness,
Thank God,
Darken the words.

Waiting for Something to Happen

Is it not enormously important,
Waiting for something to happen?

As if nothing could happen
Not unexpected,

What could happen to full nature
That has not happened before?

We sit with riches retrieved
By rich memories.

What happened before
May be as important

As what happened today,
Today love came flying,

Unexpurgated,
Undenying.

Life as a spiritual recourse,
Eruption of a spring,

Geyser weather whether
From limestone or basalt

Unpredictable as a poem,
As an element,

Waiting for something to happen
You cannot tell what will happen

Yet from improbable essences—
Of the Essenes?—

Spirit leaps up
In new idioms

Weightless as the ethereal
Comprehended by the material

It is as if suddenly love
Is what man can dream of.

Quantum mechanics
Our dynamics,

Which states the irrational
Passional.

Face in the Clouds   Larger Than Life Size

I saw a face in the clouds,
The genius of the skies,
At sunset over vast ocean
And said to my neighbor

Do you see the face in the clouds?
He said he discerned the great features,
As of an artist of the universe,
Embodying ideas ever had

Of superior intelligence, eternal spirit,
Features of nobility and restraint,
The claim of supernatural personality
Dominating nature's impersonality,

But what would you expect? In
Ten minutes the great real image in the skies,
Something to make mankind feel grand,
Was smudged out by change, as night came.

II

The face I saw in the skies
Reminded me something of Keats
But greater than Keats, far greater,
A face of hundreds of thousands of miles

Suggesting the dreaming quality of space,
The quality of dream of time,
A vastness which Keats would applaud
As the clench of sensuality,

The senses superbly felt above the earth
In a crescendo of immediate faith
In imagination as nearest to the godhead,
Beneficence so grand as to be kind

And as the vision grew and remained static
There was no sense of chaos or of anxiety,
Yet such images breed their own dissolution,
The face of humanity watered away to its vanishing.

To see an anthropomorphic god in the skies
In the face of a man, was to experience spirit
Inadmissible to the intellect and to reason.
It means that man yearns for something beyond himself

And when he sees, in instantaneous intake,
The veritable beneficent face of ultimate reality
He is astounded, cannot find words for it
And makes poetry in place of religion,

The sight that he saw become insight,
The face a mask of greater reality and time
And space resolving itself to infinitude,
Before dream withdraws its presence, and ends.

Then man becomes the struggle again,
Asking himself the old questions of reason,
He cannot uphold a heavenly, too skyey glimpse,
Thinks it was a hoax, falsehood, a cosmic joke.

The Flag

The flag was a fabric to wave in victory,
Hold up in defeat.
It was the symbol of the tribe,
Tribe nationalism.

When World War II was raging
Each side held up its particular flag.
As millions were dying
Which side was God on?

We held ours at Iwo Jima,
A picture of belief.
Lee held his up at Bull Run.
All wars are man's defeat.

Song

I see her in her feeble age,
Aunt Nellie Morris,
I see her at eighty years of age,
Aunt Nellie Morris,
Picking at asters on the pillow grass,
With a broken hip bone in a plaster cast,
Her mind gone, her bones wobbling,
Feverish to get up and go downstairs.

I see her in her frolic youth,
Aunt Nellie Morris,
I see her at eighteen years of age,
Sweet Nellie Morris,
Delighting to ride from the village to the town,
Eager to purchase a new Easter hat,
The world is equal to her vast appetite
At one remove from the charts and stamps.

Eighty years of life, death any hour now.
What does it come to? what does it go to?
Death; words, words to sing of death:
Love to proffer sweet Aunt Nellie Morris,
Out of the feverish animal and wretched bed,
Out of the skies of water and lands of air
Where nor hand nor eye nor lips nor mind
Enter. Calm is but the end of a poem.

Sea Storm

Evening at the calm,
That's the best of all.
The seas quiet enough to think.
Not to have to combat them.
They are so much stronger than
Man they could kill him.
He survives, and triumphs, for a time,
By chance and wit. Wit to foresee
The fall of the barometer,
The danger of old charts,
Too many aboard,
Lack of ship-to-shore CB,
Lack of a young mariner
In case old ones
Have a heart attack,
The sea
Is not interested
In the pleasures of summer folk.

Evening at the calm,
If it would only stay still
Like this,
The full tide coming in
With a slight breeze,
The tide extraordinarily full
Under a full moon in July,
The moment of stasis
I praise,

I could tell you tales of the sea
And will tell you one.
At four o'clock
On an August afternoon
With a heavy southwester blowing,
Timmy Rhodes appeared,
A calm man on the coast of Maine,

Owner of Beach Island down Penobscot Bay,
And said,
Would you take me out in *Reve*,
My son may be lost in the storm.
He left Beach Island in the morning
In a slight dinghy with an outboard,
Has not been seen since.
He may be washed up on an island
Between Beach and the mainland,
Will you go search for him?

We knew there was not much light left.
We said sure, let's go. Timmy and I, and
Jackson Brodsky, six feet six, and our dog,
Boarded the cruiser *Reve* in heavy weather,
I with misgivings, but hopeful to find Timmy's son,
And took off toward Spectacle Island.
We searched the shore, found no body or boat.
We headed for Fiddle Head and Hog Island,
The seas were high but still island-repulsed.
We searched Hog and Fiddle Head.
When we got beyond Hog heading for Beach Island
The full weight of the storm bore on us,
From the West over the Camden Hills,
To left and right a hundred miles of ocean
Came at us in a red ominous light of sun
And man-chewing fury.
We took the seas on our starboard quarter.
Half across
Tons of water crashed into the after cockpit,
Fortunately self-bailing,
Whereupon Timmy said,
With the calm of an old New Englander,
"I wouldn't let that happen again."
I had heard the phrase about
Shivering the timbers. *Reve*'s timbers shivered,
She rose up and shook off the heavy waters
Piling over her and into her,
One stood fast at the wheel, all one could do.
I plied the cruiser like a sailing vessel,

Turning her into the highest waves,
Searching out any point of vantage,
We had faith in our vessel,
But knew to expect any eventuality.
The red sea in all its might and selfhood,
A deadly sight of malevolent oncome,
Total affront, how could we survive this,
Yet we kept on through the forcing waves
At low speed, and came to Beach Island
Where the storm was so strong,
The waves so high, we could not
Pick up a mooring, had to
Head her into the wind,
Keep the engine going, keep her
Head on, direct against danger of sidestroke,
And how long could we do this?

Timmy, fearful for his son,
Wanted to get off,
Go by dinghy to Lisa Jane,
Insisted he would not give up
But search the islands for his son.
We didn't think he could get off,
How he got off I'll never know
But he did, and rowed to Lisa Jane,
Took off in lording seas to find his son.
We might never see him again.

Now the light was leaving, we had
Only about an hour, and had to decide
Whether to seek the leeward of Beach
And anchor for the night, in the tearing,
Tear-forcing storm,
Which we knew not whether it would
Get worse or abate,
So we left perilous stasis
Of heading into the wind
And a hundred miles of red, hard-evil seas,
And got around to the lee.
It all seemed desperate.

We finally decided
That since we had crossed from Hog to Beach
And taken tons of water,
But survived,
We had better chance it again,
Get home by nightfall in half an hour
Rather than chance
A slippery anchor
And the unknown terrors of the night.

So we headed *Reve* into the storm,
Now with the wind and the waves on our port,
And tried her through the waves
Evading the big ones turning into them.
It was a poker passage but we made it,
Some lee help from Fiddle and Spectacle,
And brought *Reve* to mooring at Undercliff,
Just before dark.

The father who might have lost his son at sea,
Timmy, appeared later at Undercliff by car
From Buck's Harbor, with his tall son, who,
His motor conked out, took off his shirt and
Made a sail in the dinghy and in the high wind
And seas, a young man sure of himself, fearless,
Sailed into Buck's Harbor miles away,
Hardy and able, evading death, even happy,
And Timmy had scoured the faceless seas,
Not found his son or his boat,
And directed Lisa Jane into Buck's Harbor,
Where was his boy
Luckily out of the predation of the ghastly waters.

We had a round of drinks
To fortune,
That happened to turn out good that day.

Hopelessness of Achieving the Past

You have swum the Hellespont, climbed the Acropolis,
Walked on the Great Wall of China, addressed the Taj Mahal,
Seen wild animals at Amboseli,

Have looked on Scylla and Charybdis from Taormina,
Have walked on Mallorca to Valdemosa
From Puerto Pollensa, Chichen Itza from Merida,
Testing strength, escaping destruction,

Yet the past arises unattainable,
Elusive soul that escapes us,
Something we did not know
We thought we knew when we were experiencing

But now we are unable to pursue,
We are tricked by time
And sit in an armchair at thirty degrees below zero,
Drinking Scotch to keep the spirit warm

In the state of New Hampshire, where skiers
Leap as you did down the mountain in ecstasy,
In ability, and splendid turns and curves,
When yesterday was today, absolute and clear.

Bats

The sun is descending in the middle of July
With the greatest impersonality,
The descending light
Has a hidden eloquence.
I have thought for decades it would speak.
I sit sensing the subtle twilight
And I wish to hear the meaning of the world.

Surely the silence of the twilight
Will speak what man wishes to hear.

Surely the splendor of evening
Will have something to say.

Day was changing into night
In the same way when in youth,
As now, I loved the soft changes.

I do not know sidereal answers,
Nor earthy ones, better now.

The body changes, nature seems
And in this seeming seems the same.

The truth is that at a predictable half hour
In high summer between eight-thirty and nine
Bats by the dozens, counted up to seventy,
Will drop and take flight from small apertures
Above my study, nested in the double roof,
And wing their way in the growing darkness
Catching insects, and that the exterminator,
Supposedly versed in the supremacy of man,
Does not know how to get rid of them.
He says they will fly away in the fall,
But another expert says it may be a species,
Having found a happy home in our house,

Which will hibernate under our double eaves
To propagate their kind another summer.

Up against predestination, one way or another,
A mathematical principle
Twitters in my mind.

Belief

Hiss of a goose
Is fine on a farm,
However refined
In poets' song.

The hiss of a snake
Is likewise pure,
The snake in the grass
Makes us endure.

The howl of the wolf,
A strong relief,
Waking in the wilderness,
True as ours, his belief.

Far Out

The secret life
Is the deep secret life of everyone.
For in moments of relief,
Perhaps by music, by suffering, by joy
We see what we meant
When, dumb, we lived at our highest.

At those high points of existence,
Joys known beyond the word,
We did not know what we were doing,
But as memory releases us to significance,
We stand into immortality.
It is too great a word to be put down.

What I mean is that we cannot know
How close love brought us to the real
Until, sufferings necessarily accepting,
We have a glimpse of our high glimpses,
Immortal in the sense that they are gone,
Transiency permanent in transiency.

When we knew the ecstasies of love
We knew the ecstasies of love, great times,
But then time took away the strangeness
As it provided other kinds of strangeness,
And we were hard put to it to understand
What we could feel, what time made us do.

I do not wish to end this poem,
The secret life
Goes on unendingly, I devote my will
To aim at will-lessness, and to open
Poetry to apertive speculation,
Everything we say hard to be caught

Because we may have said or felt something
That lives in the realm of immortality
Which men do not understand, and cannot see,
We may have entered the truth, and
Unknowing, communicated directly with Buddha,
Or won a nod from cross-shouldering Jesus.

Good Place

No poetry can be Phoenix
Living only in the head,
Poetry from the head down
More resourceful
Than poetry brain-breached.
I realize
Aspirations, dreams
Tend from the head up,
And in and out of
Intellect,
While poetry of the flesh,
Which Keats knew,
And Hopkins, and Thomas,
Is a thing in itself,
Sensuousness of being,
The mind freeing,
Casting the mind
Because it never
Answered ultimate questions,
Believing in the force
Of the whole being in love,
In suffering,
Believing in the force
Of man in his totality.

Inexplicable

What is that music always in the air,
Unheard but imagined?
While you are walking along with the crowd
The subtle music overheard?

Controlling your concept of reality,
Realer than the shuffle of innumerable feet?
A music supreme and complete,
Secret secretion of the air.

When you are thrown down on a mass of graves
As you were thrown up on waves of life
There was always a music beyond you, there,
Indefinable, subtle, sweet, and rare.

Island Message

If I chose a different pen
Would this be a different poem?

If I chose a red pen
Would it be a red poem,
If a blue pen, a blue,
If a yellow, a yellow?

If I chose a chalk in Southern France
Would it be the same on a cave wall?

If I chose no pen at all,
Chose no pencil, no brush

Would the poem float in the air,
Float through my brain, senses,
Exquisite, elegant, flaunting the air,
Ultimate music never put down,

Would this be the poem of beginnings,
The poem of endings?

Think of the strength, the vitality
Of all things never set down,
Vibrant in eternal knowingness,
Alive in eternal nothingness,

O poem reaching divinity,
O poem real, abstract as God.

Could this wild sensual reality,
Like love of lovers flesh-pent,
Like dreams of young, daring poets
Ever be penned in my matrix,

Ever be wrested from soul to prosody,
Ever be caught in the maker's make?

Invisibility be my master,
Passionate acclaim be my savior,
Overwhelm me history's England,
In love with poets of her island,

Words, outlast this passionate frame,
Poems, be read beyond me,

I am one charged with accountability
And love to give my life to poetry
And never know whether a word of mine
Would excite the eye of the twenty-fifth century,

And believe in the great ineffable reaches
Of the soul full of knowledge and right,
Man who has lost glory, who has lost faith;

I call him back to great days
Of high reality, of high possibility,
Glimpse of wholeness in our night.

Key West

Is far out, umbilically extravagant.
Pelicans come in behind the shrimpers,
Tossed cutoff fish heads from the day's catch.
Dogs bark at night, cats high-pitched.
The sun is the greatest thing about Key West,
A savage source. Dangerous to the thin-skinned,
Blonds fight off its cancerous attraction
By moving to shades whose winds may cool.

Audubon's done-over house has a shady garden
With cool white iron chairs. Hemingway's house
Is more elegant than you would have thought of him,
The cat population has declined from fifty to forty-one,
Strewn placidly about, some authentic six-toed descendants.
Tennessee Williams' house is entirely closed in,
A tropical hideaway surrounded by walls.
The graveyard looks like Italy not America,
Houses run from quaint to spectacular, to old.

Order

Order, to impose order
On grief, on suffering.
Order, a triumph.
Order, the impossible.

I hear Handel playing,
The measures of the mind
Pleasing from the blood.
The stay of pleasure.

Order, I want order,
Not pain, not suffering.
Order, the solace.
Order, the dream.

I see Goya painting
Men shooting men.
The brutal statement
Triumphs by order.

When Rock was poisoned
I wept my heart out
As the disordered animal
Retching slowly died.

Order, I seek order
Within the human.
What is beyond the stars
We cannot comprehend.

Sharp of Michelangelo
To manifest David,
Mark the human
By exaggeration.

Order, to dream order,
Illogic of logic,
A flare of life
In the face of death.

The poet with a plan,
Dante, passion in control,
Steps through hell
In orderly cantos.

Order be the poise
And now the mind renew
And the heart announce
Pleasures of the day.

Salute

To Ivor and Dorothea

After the action of action, what?
Thought. Gut!
Vessel down the ways,
Baby down the sluiceways.
Gut! Thought! What?

Pot, Shot, Got, Lot.
Pillar of salt, Gestalt.
Bhagavad-Gita, here?
Buddah, better still Prince?

I threw myself into action
Acting like an actor a part.
Fool, clown, tragedian!
Riots riotous! Crotch!

After the action of action, what?
More action? More thought? More gut?
Violence! Yes, a pence.
A penny for the world's violence.

How to escape a poem?
The old glory men, Keats, Hopkins.
Negative capability,
Pied beauty.

We Americans love craze.
We will do anything.
Walt said he had children,
We are lyres all.

Seventy bats fly out
From my study, every evening.
Nature is with us! Bats!
I do not want to be the Exterminator.

Bats in the attic,
A pain in the wing,
A poem in the evening,
Lust everywhere!

Bats, hornets, toads, ants,
I love you, creatures of life,
Gorge yourselves on earth,
Winter is coming.

A Telling

"O Earth, O Earth, return!"

Life we grasp, and toss to and fro,
Alone in our being, tossing to and fro.
Rain washes away worlds of snow.
Aid comes from the wide summer's glow.
Man must reap what man must sow.
I am fated wherever I may go.
Ever is never, I come, and I go.

Who am I? We struggle years to know.
You are my love? Will I ever know?
O how winds blow over plains of snow!
Mountains hold us in, never let us go.
If I cultivate I must rake and hoe.
Now is now, ever and never, as I grow.
Going to die is as strange as to know.

Time

I still think time is the enemy,
Not man. It is because time is invisible,
Bland. You cannot give it a karate kick.
It has neither Machiavelli nor Gethsemane.

I cannot imagine time without time,
Space spaceless. They are here to stay.
Yet man may be faceless. He may ruin
Himself, be not long on the way.

I should like to challenge the seasons to stop.
It would be a gesture of absurdity,
Reckless assertion of incredibility
Would wrest me from maturity to the nursery.

The Visionary

Breathless at onset, unset, the
Stop of the heart,
What poets told long ago,
Some troubador lover,
Before the age of science,

Makes me expect grace
In the form of flesh,
Living flesh at its best,
Blessing of being,
Sanctification leading on

So that from the love of woman
I climb through a forested mountain
To a pinnacle of ice
And there I behold a clarity
That shakes me,

Vision inescapable
When love is full of life,
Life full of love dreams up
Majestic summits,
Thrilled with the idea of unity,

A new happiness of bemusement
Glimpsed in the ice pinnacle,
Glimpsed, not fully known,
Sensed in solitude, joy in the flesh,
Joy of timeless essence

Unbelieved in but believed in,
A thrust of imagination
Imagined by the senses
Given to man in a flash, a
Gash of immaterial radiance

So that mankind may see,
Despite despair of intellect,
Something fixed beyond himself,
Mankind, these times, the world,
From the love of woman

Without whom no man lived
To speculate on life and death,
Through whom, fleshly mother,
He senses wisdom
From high-frequency onset, unset.

Fog I

Fog depends on density, but so does man.
Now you can see *Reve* in the bay, with
Attendant boats, now scarcely, now you cannot.

Man depends on the density of his knowledge,
But finally it is blackout. He was bright,
But fog moved in occluding his spirit.

Pleasant to sit on the land looking at the fog
On the sea. Will it lift, or be total occlusion?
Fog moves in and out, ideas move in and out.

Fog brings on a stealthy quietude, through which
A sea bell speaks far out, or, near, a sea gull.
Quiet of earth before the storm of birth.

Total density is total invisibility.
After life, we must be in a total fog.
Forever quiet, but this won't last forever.

After some time, the clamor of high sunlight,
Far bright looks, action, the speeches of men.
In fog you thought you knew something irremediable.

Fog II

Clarity is the excellence of rationality.
Socrates in the agora was not fogged in.
Plato and Aristotle could be explicit in their ways.

We use a word like glory for clarity,
We use a word like chaos for madness,
Some great men have been mad, some sane.

If I sit in the fog, looking at the fog, not
Seeing through the fog, how clear can I be?
By imagination I can be clear as in clear sunlight.

But then, in sunlight I could be metaphorically fogged.
What, then, is the controlling principle? Nature,
Nature is the master of man, nature controls him.

I cannot ask the fog to go away, to vanish,
I cannot ask a sunny day to turn to fog,
I can ask, who am I, what am I doing in the world?

Accommodating Oneself to September

After high summer, high blood on high seas,
How can one accommodate oneself to September?
Over the waters comes a face of chagrin
Not to maintain the high, supreme tempo
But a reality of falling off
Even to the chaos of a hurricane,
Perhaps. Maybe not that dramatic a decline,

As if to say, I never understood myself,
Must blow off, shout, scream, and kill.
I must live in rage if at all,
I throw my tempestuous cruel power
At all of you frightened on the mainland,
I blow down your trees, tear up your houses,
I despise anything I cannot destroy.

After living at the height of summer
One must expect irrational storms,
Nature is reluctant to have given grace,
And takes it out on us in wrath.
Too nearly perfect to have lived days
With calm seas and high, hot afternoons
With views around the compass from Barred Islands.

I would never want to stop living
If I could keep always the vision of a love
Equal to the irrational force of nature,
A love unafraid of a hurricane,
But would lean into it at a forty-five-degree angle
And say, I understand what you have in mind,
My serene order will outlast your destruction.

How can one accommodate oneself to September?
We forget April when we accept September.
September is a green and gold mistake, said Emily.
Emily triumphed over them both by love and death.
I want to accommodate myself to September
As a father accommodates himself to a son,
Knowing there is Spring ahead to love life.

Fate's Election

Poets who flew into nothingness,
I remember them, their names are forgotten,
They leaped into truth as into high clouds,
They aspired to heavenly conjunctions,
Nothing could persuade them to nothingness,
They flung love in the face of the air,
They were tempestuous and periodic,
Bright acquirers of instantaneous belief,
They thought excitement, they crazed themselves
With sinewy essences expressing celerity,
They thought themselves the Sun itself in sunlight,

These were the poets, every one of them, whose hope
Outleaped their words, and lived high
In the realm of statements of the great poets,
They thought they existed in pure flame,
They had the irreducible human aspiration
Of a man who thinks that he knows something,
Some central part of himself inviolable,
Some truth too tremendous to be put down,
Yet these poets all of whom I remember
Are dead, they are nothing, their live hopes
Along with their lives flew into nothingness.

Great Principles Are Thrown Down by Time

You stand thinking of great principles
But they are thrown down by time.
You think your intellect holds them
But your intellect is altered by time.
Time changes, the eyes change, as fate
And the great principles go on in time.

What if Aristotle, if Plato were here?
What if they were at the Academy in New York?
Can we imagine it? Are any of our men
Able to withstand thousands of years
And enounce principles that are the great principles?
We freshen ourselves in throes of difficulty.

Yet the great principles of the live Greeks
Are thrown down by time. I heard
A commissar in Washington in 1960, when I
Got too friendly with Yevtushenko and Vosnesensky,
Discredit the entire classical Greek establishment,
Say the tragic flaw is a defunct idea,

There could be no tragedy in his country
Because all were equal, none could fall
From a high state to a low state because of a flaw
In character; like bees or ants, if numbers
Were killed numberless numbers would follow
To keep the hive or hill alive with future.

Individualism inheres in Western freedom,
Dynamism thinks it knows which way to go,
Blake, Keats and Hopkins shine alive,
Democracy's skin burnishes to one color,
If we want to know what is the matter with America
Now, we can warm our guts in the blood of Whitman.

This poem was read by the author to Vice President Walter F. Mondale at the "Spirit of the City" award dinner of the Cathedral of St. John the Divine, in New York, in December 1977.

We can feel the vitality of our striving
Here and now, in the heart-city of our land,
Can sense the visionary grandeur of our founders
In the erected freedom of our high-sprung spirits,
And when we suffer and fall, hail to America,
We have the strength to throw the evil-doers out.

Great principles are replaced by time
While the eyes see man as teeming, an upward
Animal, begetting in love, hope, and belief.
If he joins the brontosaurus, the Incas, the Aztecs
So be it, and so be it love incomplete.
With poetry he was replete.

Harmony

Any sense of harmony fills me with awe.
It is as if out of destruction, out of chaos
A saved man or woman spoke the truth,
Or woke the symphony to crescendo,
And gave harmony to the nature of man,
Too high to realize in our times,

Shootings, killings, stabbings, murders, disaster
Assailing us on every page and every day
So that we cannot imagine harmony. Grace
Is a word removed from our vocabulary.

Hour

It is the mystical hour of incredible peace
Beyond the hatreds of man and his wars,
It is that twilight hour
When the soul sees best,
A half-light, half day, half night,
A momentary splendor of peace
As real as the real brutalities
Of man the killer, the slayer, the beast,
While here is something in nature
Elevating the soul, which now is calm.

Yet two ducks hatched five ducklings,
Tiny, fluffed out in their first day,
Serene, on a small pond beside which
Man made them a house with a trap door.
On the first night of the ducklings
Raccoon hands sprang the trap door
And ate up the ducklings, all but one,
Oddly saved by whacking beaks and wing-beats
Of parents.

The Melancholy Fit

When I say these words I think of Keats
And wordless things
But he made words from it

And now the melancholy fit
Has come on me
And I have words for it

Although the term is not right
And this is another century,
I do not feel melancholy

I feel fit, and next Spring
Will have lived
Three times as long as young John.

What does this mean?
I do not know, I admit
No comparisons, my admiration

For Keats high as heaven
But what I am interested in
Is the poetic origination.

It comes in some kind of fit
But that is the wrong word
As is melancholy also.

If a fit comes to nescience
Poetry comes to flare,
A glory.

If poetry states the unstatable
So much the better for it,
And that is fit.

Necessity dictates the form.
I picked up three-by-fives,
No other paper around,

So this poem conforms to that.
Doc Williams would appreciate this,
He wrote on a prescription blank.

My prescription for life
Is poetry, take it,
Thanks, and be whole.

P.S. It blanks out the prescription
And gives the glory,
Its story, history.

New York Prospect

For Pete and Dorothy Dean

It used to be that you had a full view
Of the Old Lady,
The ships moving
Down to sea,

From your height
It was heady to see
No rift
In the French gift,

Now it is only years later
And your view,
Occluded
By shot up buildings,

Is not true,
Your view is divided
By time's upshot
On the narrows,

No doubt
In a year
You will not be able to see
The Statue of Liberty.

You will be thrown inner as we are
Admitting a New York prospect,
Admit that your view of life
Is you.

Pitch of Grief

Grief is for those who know the end
Of life. It comes to nothing at all.

The young athlete who made his name,
The young intellectual who made his fame,

The believers in the system, the disbelievers,
Those who had imagination to imagine,

The lovers of the good, the dutiful, the few,
The anarchs who never got out of anarchy,

The hopes of the mother for her son,
Of the father for rational continuance,

The rich who could not disbelieve in riches,
The poor whose mobility was poverty.

When death shakes the heart out of life,
Grief brings knowledge of nothingness.

Praise the bright eye, the dancing instep,
Hope, courage, belief, joy in action,

Youth step to youth and love,
Age bless continuance of time,

And may some dream again
Dreams of the sublime.

Talking Back to Nature

Sitting in the kitchen, with the sun going down,
It has an inhuman stability.
The fire goes out as the fire goes down.
No doubt Plato and Aristotle are looking on.
It does not matter what they thought.
No matter what I feel, the sun descends.
So silent! What is the fury of the bones?
Why should man torment himself?
If it had not gone one way it would have gone
Another. A third world will arise and go.
Man will decline and his successor ascend.
No matter what I think or feel
The sun descending in the pine trees
Looks me in the eye out of the kitchen window.
I look him back. The sun
Will win and I not talk back.

Poets, sing songs of triumph when
You realize the weight of humanity
And you confront him, speaking your desire.

To a Dead Man

You have passed
What Tennyson called the bar,

You are dead but now living
In us, your friends and companions,

You have passed
That hour

We dream of
With distaste,

Knowing it is pre-established
Beyond our dissuasion,

You are another gone
To oblivion,

Another like us
Who much discuss

The issues, but cleave
To life in tissues,

We cannot help
Being with ourselves

The living, hardy-spirited,
Dispirited,

Yet whenever you leave,
Which is ourselves leaving,

We do not know what to believe,
What to say,

We feel strangeness,
Known death's ribs,

We are active
And you are not,

We love you intemperately,
Think of you sempiternally,

Wish you well,
Wish us well,

It is fellowship
Hell-deep heaven-high,

It is our predicament
From which we are sent.

Spirits Appearing

There is a sense that spirits appear
Because the dead are so close to the living.
They are here as real as we are.
The newly dead and the long dead
Whom you first knew in childhood.

That somehow
These mysterious essences exist alive
When ecstasy comes up to finality.
Where has love gone, as the years turn?

Where is youth, that blessed your eyebrows,
Now that age begins to shrink your skin,
Your bones push outward from within,
As flesh ages the skeleton begins.

How quickly it moves to another sphere.
The fierceness of life in a thrust for power,
High imagination commanding the earth.

If you could now find language
As pure as your vision at the start
To express belief as illimitable
Love was a word you had begun to say.

Someway the dead are in our air,
Loved integers, whether new or old,
In a mystery no words can catch.
Here I am writing at a desk
Trying to reach ineluctable mystery.

Bound to the past
We are held in the present, and we think
That we have a future, some future prospect
Better than anything we have known,
Each tonight believes in each tomorrow.

If the spirits could come back to speak to us
What would they say? None has come back to say
Anything, we are the speakers of poetry,
Yet their silence is an abstract continuum
Realistic as each call in our bodies.

We cannot live without them, the spirits,
Because they are something beyond ourselves
Yet in us, which we are becoming.
Without whose wordless, space-time trace
We would be less rich, and less aware.

Waiting

O mighty, just, and impenetrable fog,
That keeps the Western airliner on the ground,

You make me think of Icarus
In the sunshine, as dark fog thickly holds around,

We'll get out of you yet, although
Baffled in the arms of time,

Waiting craftily for a hole in the skies,
Waxing for freedom to be found.

Grandson

And while I was waiting
For my grandchild to exclaim again,
I thought of my age,
And of his young sophistication.

Such high intelligence!
Such delight of life!
But what will it come to,
Death is the knife

Will part him from his predecessors
And who can say what adventure
Will open to him
The twenty-first century?

Dear three-year-old, dear man,
What can I say to you
But love and affirmation,
And my elan

In face of obstacles,
In face of death's derision,
That I was like you
Daft with vision?

Depths

Mind brooding over the waters
Is not like the waters themselves.
They evade inching intelligence,
   Keeping the oceanic.

Study the bottom of the sea,
Strange creatures walk there.
They are no stranger than we,
   Keeping the oceanic.

I do not make the tides to go,
Nor do I make them come,
They in their own motion are
   Keeping the oceanic.

Off my port a cold shark
Shows himself, fin above water,
In night. He is in the dark,
   Keeping the oceanic.

Flash my being alive
To mankind living in my time,
Going on short tenure,
   Keeping the oceanic.

Pulling Out the Vines

Today I pulled out the vines,
They had encroached on a hundred-foot pine tree

Searching up from the earth seeking more light.
I exclaim how delicately they were organized.

I faced a problem of choice and ethics.
Was it right to destroy their summer aspiration?

If I left them to grow, how far up would they go?
The tree was much too massive to be strangled.

I decided against the delicate, tendril vines,
Surprised at how easily they gave up to my severe hand.

They came off like gossamer, and I thought of the soul,
Aspiring also, and so delicate, ripped by the hand of death.

The Fisher Cat

Wildness sleeps upon the mountain
And then it wakes in an animal
And in us, and in the sophistication of city streets
And in the danger of the indifferent murder,
We see the fisher cat on the limb of the tree,
Or is it a marten, or what is this slim, fierce beast
Caught in the flashlight's glare at night in Vermont,
Ready to leap at the baying dogs?

This enemy, this ancient foe, what is he?
The unexpected beast glares down from the high branch
Ready to pounce and fills man with fear,
Some nameless fear of millions of years ago in the forest,
Or the Rift valley in East Africa
When it was life or death in an instant.

The man has a gun, the instrument that has saved him,
Without which the drama of this intense moment
Might have ended in the death of man, and no poem,
He raised his piece like a violator of nature
And aiming at the jeweled caskets of the eyes
Brought the treasure trove of brain and sport.

The beast fell to the ground, unable to comment,
His beauty despoiled that took millions of years to grow.
The dogs thrashed around a while and quieted.
The New England hunter then with his matter of fact,
Taking for granted his situation mastery, put the
Mythic beast in the back of his four wheel drive vehicle.

It has taken the scientists of the university months
To decide what kind of an animal the creature was.
The centimeters of the back molars were counted,
Books were consulted, in the end it was decided,
Not by the scientist but by the poet, that a god
Had descended on man, and had to be killed.

Wildness sleeps upon the mountain
And when it wakes in us
There is a perilous moment of stasis
When savagery meets equal savagery.
The long arm of man maintains intelligence
By death: his gun rang out instant doom.
The paws of the animal were very wide,
The claws of the beast were wide, long his thrashing tail.

Vignettes

From Washington to New York
By air to visit earthy Robert
In the offices of Holt, there were
Marianne Moore and Robert Frost
Sitting on a divan looking good.
I admired them so much
I kept my distance.
So near, and yet so far.

When I was in college Edna
Millay read, in a red gown,
Blond hair trailing. When she walked
Out we trailed after, panting.
We thought we possessed her,
She possessed us. Behind us her husband,
A small man with a black satchel.
We thought very little of him.

I went from Cambridge to London
To see Lawrence at his picture exhibit.
He had a red beard, gesticulated
Intensely in the next room.
His paintings were red, round, womblike.
The air was electric, but smoky.
In the arrogance of my youth
I watched, did not go up to meet him.

Sitting beside Yeats one night in Dublin
With A. E. at Gogarty's, he drew
Fingers through his long gray straight hair,
Talking, frustrated, of the Censorship Bill.
When we left we walked through the fog
Blocks. He said nothing, in thought.
When we came to a certain corner,
He went one way, I went another.

A. E. put me into trance in his office
Afternoons when he would spin Indian mythologies
In the most mellifluous voice I ever heard.
He would talk of the gods as real, ancient
Time as if now, it was pure poetry.
And on Sunday nights at his house, late,
If coaxed, he would bring out his paintings,
Each of a mysterious woman, white, among dark trees.

James Stephens was incredibly short,
His head large, a light on the world,
And at the Literary Club for luncheon
He would regale fellows with torrential humor
So liquid it was intoxicating,
And then we would walk to Miss MacNie's
Where his wit was unquenchable.
Into the night we drank gallons of whiskey.

Q. let us doff our gowns at evening class
In Aristotle. We few, we happy band of brothers,
Might be asked to elucidate a line of Greek
From the *Poetics*. The gentle elder appeared,
Preceded by a butler bearing port and cigars
On a silver tray. Q. stood before the great fire,
Looking like a man from an earlier time,
And if we were lucky he would digress on Shelley.

When Eliot and Richards received their degrees
The day Marshall announced the Marshall Plan,
At Ivor's and Dorothea's cocktail party
Dorothea asked me to bring over a chair.
Billy James, son of William, had just vacated
It. He backed back and crashed on the floor.
We all gasped fearing broken bones. He got up
Smartly and said long ago he had stroked the Harvard crew.

After Dylan Thomas' reading in New Lecture Hall
Before the Advocate room on Bow Street filled up
With cocktail takers, he met a girl in décolleté
With her tuxedoed escort. He said, in a loud voice,

"Well, as for me I would rather suckle at those teats
Than go back to that old wife of mine in Wales."
Harvard shook for a week. The girl, five years later,
A mother, enjoyed Dylan's blast in retrospect.

That evening, at Matty's on Louisburg Square,
Dylan lurched up satyrlike from a rug,
Bumped a rude shoulder into the grandfather clock,
The critic's face aghast. It tottered, but settled.
Later, at the Wilburs', excess bred hilarity
In spirited tones of innocent orgiastics
Until Dylan and I had to go to the bathroom
And there we found ourselves, odd fellows apart,

Standing up together to the call of nature,
Arms around each other's shoulders, excitedly
Protesting love for each other's poetry,
True joy, as we micturated into the same bowl.
Very late the Guest House door was opened
By a frail old lady named Mrs. Tremble.
Charlee and Betty got Dylan upstairs, pulled off
His pants, and put him to bed like a baby.

Auden, with books sprawled on the floor, was writing poems
Often, it was the time of "Voltaire at Ferney" and "Housman,"
In slippers, and drinking tea with endless talk.
If I suggested an emendation he would enter it
In the freedom of an intensely free mind, and
Then put on Berlioz and turn it up grandly loud.
Once, at Sunday breakfast, he put a pill before my place,
Said, "Take this." I refused. Benzedrine. Such innocent days.

We were dining at Mrs. Granville Gordon's oast house.
She was short, elderly, charming, and widowed.
I noted a quaint English custom that the men
Did not move when she got up to feed the fire.
Probably Bill Empson, Kathleen Raine, and John Davenport were
    there.
Timothy White in plaid waistcoat, flamboyant jacket,

Took out gaudy red stuff and two long, white, ivory knitting
    needles
Knitting for hours while we talked, before the fire.

Manny Forbes had great Sunday morning breakfasts at Clare,
Which went on into the afternoon. He exposed Blake
In class with many colors of chalk explaining poems.
And when he built "Finella" across the Backs
He had a bathroom done all in shining black,
Mythical Celtic figures on the ceiling in the dining room.
He asked Epstein to set up his statue of Eve,
Asked students to pay a shilling to come and see her.

Poets came to our house for the Inauguration of Kennedy.
Tate, Lowell, and Auden were there, Auden bustling
Socially in the kitchen, helping with the dinner.
Katherine Anne Porter, Madame Perkins, the founder
Of Social Security, and a woman first to go to Russia
With George Bernard Shaw, talked animatedly.
The weather was slushy. Katherine Anne said,
"But I have only my little red slippers." Auden stayed home.

The slush and mud at the Ball were Jacksonian.
We usurped a vacated cubicle, drank free champagne,
And danced, in the crowd, before the President and Jackie
Feeling a great lightness and a new light
Shining over the United States of America.
After one o'clock old Robert Frost slowly stalked
Across the floor, moving with uncertain ease but strong,
Climbed up, and sat on a dias with dignitaries.

The day after the inauguration of President Kennedy
We went to a cocktail party at the Coxes,
Neighbors in Georgetown near 34th Street.
The Hindemiths were there, I had not known composers,
The talk was all of the new America.
Robert Frost was there. I went up to him eagerly, saying,
"I hear you talked with the President this morning,
What did he say?" Instant reply, "I did all the talking."

Long ago, after a reading at the Y,
We repaired to Howard Moss' in the village.
Soon the room was veil-filled with smoke.
Far across a pair of eyes like flashlights held me.
Soon this young man was sitting at my feet,
He had no name. He said my poetry so moved him
He was thrown to ecstasy in the mental hospital,
Then back a notch, relapsed. He became Allen Ginsberg.

Once by the Pacific Betty, Marie, Kenneth and I
Were driving northward high over the ocean, Kenneth
Was driving. We were talking of love, of pacifism.
All of a sudden a spectacular bird, a red bird
Flew by the front of the car quite near.
Rexroth let go the wheel, excitedly began
Giving a lecture. I feigned needing to make a stop,
Came back, and took the wheel away from him.

In 1952 I was sitting in my offce, in Seattle,
When in came the F.B.I., truculent and bristling.
Did I know a poet named William Carlos Williams?
He had written a subversive poem called "The Pink Church"
In which he called the Russians comrades. Weren't they?
We were shoulder to shoulder in the war. I said he was
As good an American as they were or I was,
Investigate America, go back and read his poetry.

Once at Yaddo with Roethke for a month and a half
He came down to dinner boyish in a new suit.
Before that in his room he had burst out of the bathroom
Stark naked, a big bear smiling, waving a towel.
One weekend I drove a party over to Bennington,
We all got drunk, the Nemerovs were there.
Later I drove Ted to Boston in the rain.
We talked into sandwiches, looking East.

One time four of us were at a bar in Saratoga
Springs, Ted was pounding on the table for his drink,
Impatient because the waiter wouldn't bring it.
He flew into a frenzy of vocal rage, quite

Unreasonably, and we all had to calm him down.
He was wildly threatening the man behind the bar.
I thought if he got out of his fantasy and attacked him
He might well have had his knock blocked off.

At Yaddo I remember Bill Williams writing "Paterson."
I had the next studio and across the vernal silence
Little clicks would come. I would go over for lunch
And Bill would pull a piece of paper from the typewriter,
Read it to me clearly to see how it would go.
For days it would be the same, the clicking
Stitching the silence with newest meaning.
He was keen to proffer friendship everywhere.

To see Wallace Stevens walking down Hilliard Street
Was unforgettable. He came to see the Yale game
Each year, and sat at the top of the stands, surveying
From a height the to and fro of victory and defeat,
Then he would sit in our large leather armchair,
Amiable and kindly. Before I took him to his last reading
I showed him the Gropius new architecture, then passed the red
    bricks
Of the old law school. He said, "Why can't they make
    something as good as that?"

Diffident, Robinson Jeffers declined,
Then said to come early in the day, he knew me.
When we arrived by the tower and house,
A tall old man with one walleye
Came out pulled by a bulldog on a long chain.
In the kitchen, tea and no talk.
A slow friendship developed, he showed us
His study, then finely talked of poetry.

Once with Lowell aboard *Reve* going down
Eggemoggin Reach talking fast about poetry
We dodged lobster pots crossing Jericho Bay,
Turned right at Egg Rock, still talking fast,
Soon found a wrong marker, low hills ahead,
Suddenly bemused and in a kind of fright.

We were 180 degrees in error,
Poetry had overwhelmed reality.

Turning around and silencing the talk
We were now headed for Blue Hill Bay,
Far off the greater hills of Mount Desert,
Which had seemed in my eyes the truth
But were in fact the lesser heights of Ile au Haut.
When you are in a vessel heading northeast
Yet find you are actually going southwest,
You may have gone crazy for love of poetry.

Would I bring him a fifth of gin from Bangor?
He was allowed to have a teaspoon daily,
A frail man of ninety, with a tansy voice,
He used to call me "dear" sometimes, Maine-wise.
He made knives from steel files; with patience
You might get some by the end of summer.
His wife died. One summer he was not there.
Gook Bakeman reported him in the hospital.

I drove by this summer in real surprise.
There was no sign of Mr. Snowman's shack.
These two people have been obliterated.
Their house and shop have been obliterated,
Not a trace left: green grass growing.
I could wish for their friendly old greetings,
The fine cutting edge of a Snowman knife.

Mr. Lord-Rousseau was small, and round, and gleeful.
A carpenter by choice, he whittled winters
Awkward dolls, a lion out of this world,
His Indians were superb, about six inches tall.
His cackling wife was brittle as a whittle,
His birds were free, remain flying standing.
In painting he confected gigantic waterfalls
With tiny men with great fishhooks beneath them.

His carving hands were finally carved
Into a mockery of the things he made,

Regenerative Mr. Rousseau-Lord degenerated
When he was ninety, his round body cradled.
By ninety-two he did not know you,
Smiled affably undressing, and died in a creep.
We inhabit a world of the unknown Lord.
We inhabit a world of the unknown Mr. Lord.

എ§ F O U R §െ

Memory and Desire

So green was a hill in China once
I thought I would never love so green a thing,
It was beyond sense. One could only sing!
My sense was young to that purity
Of a green hill seen from the China Sea.
I can never hold in my hand that green.

You have heard me tell of that purity
Of death which it is man's hope to probe.
But he can never come up to it and live.
It is ever beyond him in the grave.
I contemplate death to merit spirit,
But wish to live in the hearts of men.

I seek a symbol for all natural power,
Not needing a symbol, having power in sight:
Three bald eagles wheeling over Undercliff.
I was so astounded, my heart so raved,
So pent I was with everything I love,
I think I should like to be an eagle in the light.

Spirit Descends in Man

Man is a block of wood
Of the finest grain, hard
Wood. He grew up in the forest.

Suddenly an ax struck the wood,
Splitting it in half.
It was lightning from heaven.

The lightning revealed his soul,
Which was forever dichotomous.
Two blocks fell to the ground,
One was flesh, one spirit.

The Interrogator

As the last leaf on the tree
Will you say something about the great one?

    I object to being the last leaf.
    And he was not all that great.

But the fact is that you are the last one.
The others have all gone into the world of night.

    I cannot bear an arbitrary burden.
    I am who I am, as was the great one.

The great one could not live alone,
Had to have a social group around him.

    I repeat that I am myself alone.
    I recognized him, but I love myself.

You have to say what the great one means
Before it is too late to assess him.

    Let the tree die and the great one with it.
    I refuse to give up my identity.

The Long Swing

I miss the long swing
Under the great tree,
Which reminded me
Of my youth.

Back and forth,
Forth and back
I went in the long swing
In my age,

Upheld by a giant branch,
Like the son of a father.
The swing was metrynomic,
The present whole and all.

Grace and charm,
The slow, long glides,
Blood's harmony,
Sense of long love.

Division

Division, malice of time,
Time divides us. We were whole,
But something intervened,
It was decades of the sun coming up,

Of the sun going down. It was the moon
Impersonal after being stepped on.
It was the lashing laugh
Of time, grand killer.

A small boy comes into the kitchen,
Full of life and energy,
He is just beginning to talk,
He has lived more than two years.

His face beams like an unfallen angel.
What can he learn from the grown?
Time will pack knowledge into him,
Sequestering, the minimal, come later.

Eroding comedy. Life zipping,
Only captured by art. Art changing,
Poetry problematical.
If we love, at least we love.

If we do not love, at least we live.
If we are suicidal, if we are not,
Substantiated, the joke,
Time, eradicative.

The Challenge of the Air

Air, what are you doing to me?
I am more sensitive to you
Than you are to me.

I assume glory,
You supply dust.

You can ruin
The lives of millions,

You are like our mother:
She leaves us motherless.

A poem is supposed to have
Form.

You have no Form
But you have Reality.

I can change the form of a poem,
I cannot change the form of the air.

If we pollute you,
You spit back harder.

Dear air, how I love you!
If it weren't for you
I would be loveless!

How can I do anything
Without your loveless love?

Even though you kill me
I love you.

Love you, you are life itself,
(You steel me to steel)

Later my poems will accuse you

That you are unfair
And that you obstructed

My glorious advance to truth.

I called for pure air,
You answered dust, rust.

No Control

How can we acquire a taste
For stability
When the weather shows an ability
For changeability?

It changes from hot to cold
In a day or less,
And whether to sweat or freeze
Is anybody's guess.

I have to salute the weather, whether
Cold or hot,
Man is worsened by his fate
Whether he is alive, or not.

Classification

Where was Heaven but in the afterthought
Of Heaven. Heaven was impossible.
We are in a lesser place. The dark
Darkens us to impossible darkness.
We do not like to think of it. Then what?
Another day between Heaven and Hell,
Or call it the dark, hearkens us to labors
Of quotidian exercise. Every man, woman, and child
Lives in the mid-kingdom of the here and now.
What joys! what sorrows! what eventual fallings-off,
As the sun rises and the sun sets,
As the media tells us the news,
We think the mind will control the universe,
We think to convert nature to pleasure,
We don't think we will drop the atom bomb,
I read Angelus Silesius,
Transported back, and wonder what
He would think of our century
And what,
Centuries hence,
Anyone would think of us?
Comedy greater than tragedy,
The comic mind sees a tragic joke
In the mutterings of the universe,
In the sense that I say what I am,
For pretty soon I will be not
And the whole theory will be shot.

Throwing Yourself Away

It is this continuous throwing yourself away
Suggests the clarity of the new. You divest yourself
Of relationships past and present
Because they get in the way of revolutionary
Ego, and when you have faced the deep ego
You think of the true. Then what will you do?

It is essential to throw yourself away.
If you hold on to the past,
You will be locked in a vise
Without springing relationships,
Whereas if you throw away the past, beginnings
Accrete. You think you can live anew.

And then you think you can speak of the true.
But how? You are now a more new, revolutionary
Ego, bent on capturing the flight
Of the seagull, devoted to circumlocutions
Of the dolphin, knowing the life animals
And birds allow. You close with nature.

You are still forced to throw yourself away
To find song. You have penetrated abruptions,
And listed with the vessel before sinking.
You cannot unmask ancient history
But think that you can tell glory
Coming, truth's peek, before new song.

How to Make Something of the Rocks

Coming back to the coast
Seeing the rocks inflamed with little light left,
Beside the ocean tender in the declining light,
The strength of the rocks in the color of speechlessness,

I could not speak of the strangeness and the wonder,
The vastness and the power, the closeness and the grip
Of light of nature on my eyes wide open perceptive
To the invitation of ultimate wordlessness.

What I have to say is ultimately no-worded,
What I feel is a passion so deep
As to be passionless, a strength so strong
As to be weak, a belief beliefless.

Yet I cannot believe what I have said
Because, when I saw the rocks alive
With light at the end of day, I felt
There is something beyond materiality,

The ancient rocks have become immaterial,
And the late light insubstantial,
And I, I am drifted beyond corporeality
To a realm that is strange and new.

All that I have thought, all that I have known,
All that I have learned, is unable
In my transient realization
To explain this strangeness, and this newness.

The Fight against the Inert

I fight against the inert because
I am not inert, my flesh
Fresh with another day, dynamically
Intwines with vines

And with kine, their bovine breath,
The vegetable and the animal kingdoms,
I feel that I am one with vegetables,
And with animals, thus with mankind,

The inert is the ancient heaviness
Of the earth, say it is a stone,
Or a boulder standing in the garden,
An affront to every breath I breathe,

How do I cope with the inert?
I love the dim silence of the stone
And some say even stones breathe,
Subtle brothers to us in our breath.

Fresh, high sky, incredibly brilliant,
Fills me with delight, and delicate thoughts
Triumph in my make-up, my psyche,
As I arise above the inert stone to being.

I think it is the purity of my being
Baffles the inert to state that I escape it
As I soar in the great hope of man
To capture his spirit while he is living,

I shall ask no help from exemplars,
l shall name no great poet of the past,
Nor ask a pat from the dead, nor a tone
From stone, nor words from the sphinx,

To arouse me from the totality of the inert.
From the totality of the inert
I only exclaim that I was hurt
By being, by suffering life,

And I state that I am true to life,
Its rehearsing unblessing,
And that I oppose to the inertness of the stone
The mysterious dynamism of the soul.

How Do I Further Spend My Glory?

How do I further spend my glory
With time running out, new worlds being born?
   As time states me insensate,
Why should I depict the bill of a song bird?

Yet, I would spend all the glory that I have,
However useless time may make me.
   As time runs my fate
I will annunciate, and give away glory.

Let new worlds be born, I can bear them.
If mine were scintillating, brazen,
   They can bear my weight.
New times may strike a note of vainglory.

While things worsen, let me sing strong.
The center may shift, not fall apart.
   Why should the world mismate,
I not further spend my glory?

Why should I like to be defeated
When out of my arm at any moment
   May come passion so intemperate,
That I will further spend my glory.

A Rich Kiss

Perhaps,
But no perhaps about it,

Adrienne Rich
Gave me the subtlest kiss

I had,
A touch to the cheek

As delicate as soul,
Whatever that is,

A touch like the feel
Of the immortal,

Thinner than air,
Fine as infinity,

Because a dead friend
Was there in the coffin,

I was alive with dread
Of that bed,

I spoke a poem of the dead
Over the box to the living

Then, tears raining
A river of severance

I received
A rich kiss

From Adrienne Rich,
Ethereal as poverty,

The death of every living being,
And until today

I have been unable to say
It was clinch and cinch, merci.

Lilac Feeling

Scent of the lilacs instills insouciance,
They gave to the daylight;
   This scent held onto air
   Like the poet's stare.

It was too sensual to rule,
And did not;
   Already the fragrance dies,
   As it reifies.

But at least they came late
Up here in the cold country;
   As we clip their tops
   We think time stops.

Co-operation Is No Competition

Where is the cataclysmic society
That will live for love not hate
In a revolution of the mind
Beyond the nature of our state

So that competition will be lost
To children and to men, and all
Will learn co-operation instead,
Reverse the fate of man, the fall

Will be truly as a myth instead
And all those battles, blood and death
Seem a bad dream of the past,
The rewards of lack of insight

But if we love and co-operate
We may yet live to see a day
Of strength, of joy, of certainty.
It depends upon the imprinting.

If we can imprint in animals
And birds co-operation, not fighting,
It might just be that by
Imagination man could get it right.

A Token

I hold in my hand a small stone
Nature has shaped like a fish.

Millions of years it took,
Temperamental, too, for a fish look.

After the millionth wash,
Heatings, freezings, tides of today,

It was ready for my hand to pick it up,
Small rock almost exquisite.

Slippery little fish,
Hard as the mind to catch.

How It Is

Then the eighty-year-old lady with a sparkle,
A Cambridge lady, hearing of the latest
Suicide, said to her friend, turning off
TV for tea, "Well, my dear, doesn't it seem
A little like going where you haven't been invited?"

Louise

Her ashes were thrown on a shrine in Japan,
Some on Montclair, New Jersey, some on California.
It is the new way to go.
We can love our friends everywhere!

Inside her skull
She was in one place for seventy years.
Her mind was rich, her body delivered dividends.
Even her ashes carry a wry smile.

As We Go

The glory fades from the world,
The light descends from the sky
That was high in the eye, mighty and believed,
We lived surcharged with faith
That our lives were continuous,

A glimpse of Ideality,
A glimpse of Paradise,

We felt Plato and Shelley,
Some high principle of extreme order,
Something we could never find words for,
As if aspiration and fact were one,
Ancient efforts of man to exceed himself,
We have come a long way,
The rose window
Of Mallorca hidden like dream,

The light descends in the eye,
And in the heart also,
Unanswerable light,
We fall into truth
And it is dark.

Understanding of the Impossible

Now that you are dead, and gone to Nippon,
And part of you scattered on Montclair,
And part of you scattered on Claremont

What am I to say who have lived
Beyond you in the real world of flesh and blood
When you have achieved spiritual particularity,

Which is to say a vagueness impossible
To conceive, that you are no more, but are
More of the same in my total memory,

Not only in poetry do you exist,
The rest is scattered ashes, now
Your wealth is less than a penny

And all our decades came to this,
That you are dead and I am living,
You in the matchless perfection dreamed of

By all those who had to think of death
And had to construe something from it
Beyond the inexactitudes of our being,

I in the penumbra beneath living light
Seen by a man, puff-brained Dante,
Who held to a boyish dream of Beatrice,

The only word to say is mystery,
Your vivid real life, now your nonbeing,
My lust to know, in the fault of not knowing,

And who can imagine Taormina in spring,
When we were young, exact, believing,
Dared to look down on Scylla and Charybdis?

And who can bring back mirth and headiness,
When everything turns, it is true, to folly,
You dead, I living, no more loving,

And what is the use, after all, of insisting
That there is something more to living
Than the moment, ungrieving, when we were moving?

Touch and Go

Writing is my meat and drink.
It is by writing that I think.
I eye (Aye, Aye) the seraphic,
Momently love Herrick.

When I was Romantic
I was frantic.
Too much yearning,
Too much burning.

My Classical
Was lackadaisical,
Too hard to do,
Not too true.

It is some deity
Of our society
I'm after, earth-riddle
Somewhere in the middle.

Going to Maine

Going to Maine is a state of mind,
Like everything else.
You may have been on Guemas Island,
In the State of Washington,

Viewing the Cascades wide over water,
Watching an eagle soar,
Impressed with the quantity of water,
And eaten bear steak with the McCrackens,

But when you return to ancient New England
The first question asked on Main Street,
With breathless expectation, is,
Are you going to Maine?

Are you going to Maine, oh,
Are you going to Maine?
And I say, yes, we are going to Maine,
And they say, When?

They want an ultimate answer
To an ultimate question.
Pestiferously human,
As if to infestate inner skin,

They question, almost with a triumph,
When are you going to Maine?
As if you were going to Heaven
And they would see you there!

And you say, yes we are going,
Harsh to be indefinite,
Yes, we are going, we are going,
Yes, we are going to Maine.

Spite Fence

After years of bickerings

Family one
Put up a spite fence
Against family two.

Cheek by cheek
They couldn't stand it.
The Maine village

Looked so peaceful.
We drove through yearly,
We didn't know.

Now if you drive through
You see the split wood,
Thin and shrill.

But who's who?
Who made it,
One side or the other?

Bad neighbors make good fencers.

Survivors

Superior elan
Sometimes offends.
One cannot stand it.
To be clear

In mind and body,
Dominating
A scene at eighty-eight

Makes one think
Too much
On height elan,
Abateless ability,

Breaks reality
Into a special claim
On the nature of man,
Especially of women

Who live longest,
Sometimes an eagle-gilt eye
Surveying the scene
From elan,

Elan's proud claim,
Gives dismay
If humility
Exists,

And if it does not,
Gives dismay
Anyway,
Because

The people suffer,
Have credible
Troubles,
Real heartbreak,

And death comes too soon
To any of them,
These sufferers,
Lauded commoners,

Yet ancient ladies,
Graceful, elegant-pictorial,
Eke on,
Drive from Boston to Maine

At ninety,
Play golf at ninety
At Castine,
A way from sorrow,

It is no ambage
To see these etched beings,
Who have evaded ill
By some mysterious principle

We do not know,
High-spirited,
They spring me
Into empathy

With those who have suffered and lost,
With imperfection,
The common lot,
Nature ruthless,

But the theme of this poem
Is that nature is
Not ruthless to them,
Seemingly,

To have joy at ninety,
Ability to drive a car
Three hundred miles without fatigue
Ought to be celebrated.

I am bemused,
I have seen too much love
Gone wrong,
Lives wasted by time,

Am challenged
By too much
Goddess control,
I cannot accept

That to live long means truth
When I think
Of Keats, of Hopkins,
Of Dylan Thomas.

"I hope to see you next year"
Comes across the bay,
A common report
Carried across the water

On an evening still and full
Of falling sunlight by the ocean.
Of course we do
We all do,

We want five chick swallows
In a nest
Under the areaway
To prosper,

And as the mother and father
Gather bugs
And stuff them
In yellow mouths

We watch the process
Until one day
Five swallows
Take their maiden flight.

They make it
Up to the rooftree,
Sit there expectant,
While mother and father

Fly in to feed them
Still; the next night
They retreat
Near the nest,

Bunched five in a row,
Fed still,
A revelation,
How splendid.

Even after mid-July,
The full moon,
The parents feed the young,
Teaching them to fly.

The laws of nature
Are from ancient time,
Why then
Not salute

Old ladies full of grace
Who have
Outwitted time,
Or so it seems,

Continue sportively
Guessing, truthward, at
Genes, environment,
Will, and chance.

Sea Bells

The pleasantry of the sea bells, and I talk to myself alone.
Evening calm, calm seas, peace gives me to myself alone.

Quintessential freedom, freedom to be silent as a shell,
A white scallop, once living virile in the sea, my ash tray,

A rest as in music, a light cessation, why has brief eventide
So strong a hold on my spirit, as does the far sea bell?

The sea bell is better than speech, a universal, one sound
As against restless particularities of our tongues.

The sea bell is a secret message of the universal,
And while designed to warn mariners in the fog,

To give them comfort, set and tended by the Coast Guard,
The sea bell seems to me a spell and urgency of incantation,

Something far out, inexpressible loneliness,
Human-spirited. It tells the nature of the ocean,

Now silent, now restive, now roused to heavy recurrence,
An enlivening, a slumbering, a reminder, a savior.

Ships are aware of the strong, oceanic sea bells,
Aids to navigation; the soul needs them too.

If we could hear the sound of immortality,
Beyond thought, beyond reach, we should be quickened,

But to hear from the shore in rich eventide
Sea bells, they remember Homeric sailings and incertitudes,

Oceanic destructions, tempests, and safe landfalls.
Hearing them, year to year, I talk to myself alone.

Man and Nature

High June late afternoon sun
Lights our house, trees, lawn
With decades-undiminished power,

Yet flesh and bones are gravitating.
Shall I shake my fist at nature
Like Beethoven, who died anyway?

I pit my strength against nature
With love and weakness, nature lasts,
But, hardy, cannot say a word.

Words are my nature, and in words
I hope to assess the glide of June
By telling nature what it is like.

I make the poet's amnesty song
Between permanence and transiency,
As if man were the master of nature.

Fog I

Fog may be total or partial or light.
When it is total, without wind or waves,
It is less dangerous than with wind or waves.

Off Dog Island in total fog with ten aboard
Dikkon hit a lobster pot. Experience
Stopped the motor instantly. He threw out the anchor.

The vessel was not likely to drift down on the island.
He put the ladder over the stern, drew breath,
Dived under the vessel with enough eyesight to see,

Assessed the situation, came up for breath,
Four immersions allowed him to free the line
Wrapped around the propeller, and to ascend,

Professionally done in cold water without a knife.
They hoisted the anchor, penetrated impenetrable fog,
Made it to safe mooring on Cape Rosier.

Fog II

The implications of fog are enormous.
If you cannot see, what can you see?
The idea of the blindness of mankind.

The father says to the son, do not go.
It is foolhardy on the ocean to go in the fog.
Mariners in Maine have deep respect for the fog.

The son says to the father, I am young.
You always told me not to go in the fog,
But when I returned you praised my ability.

The son went through the impenetrable fog
Because he was young, in some way foolishly.
The young mariner loved a sense of adventure.

The young wrest control from their elders
And take their lives in their hands on the sea,
The elders wait, hope they will make it to shore.

Transformation

The itch to be creative, to create,
Is never to be satisfied with life as it is,

As if nothing were stationary enough to stay
But the mind quickly moves it to another way,

Even when day lilies, irises, and lilacs
Capture the blessings of a keen June day

The imperious eye wants more than it sees,
Takes in the wholeness of life, but cannot

Be content, immediately intuiting an other where,
Sees something new looking through the clearest air.

What is this mysterious dynamism, distance
Placed on the here, on the now placed a future,

What does the creator want to create from the created,
Does he feel reality with reality cannot be equated,

That there is another reality which must be his moving up
Which must reject the world to make a world of his own

And why should the insistence of this creative mind
Insist on his seeing, as if true seeing were blind.

Certainly the June afternoon is without seeming parallel,
As if it were an absolute good in an absolute world

Of space and time never to be duplicated, flowers
Prominent to the eye in the splendor of the hours,

And strangely singular in the enticement of the grasses,
Unique and perfect as sensation quickly shows and knows,

Why should the creator reject the reality of nature
To reconstruct nature in some other stature?

He is enticed to a world of new time, new space
By very action of reflecting the world's true face,

The itch in the blood of man builds new prospects
Because things as they are is what he rejects,

He sees Odysseus in a man walking down the street,
He sees Saul turning into Paul, he sees St. Brendan

Crossing the Atlantic in seven years in a skin boat,
Sees and feels a new society beyond old tyranny,

He refuses to see the summer garden as it is
As becoming something else than it was or is,

Transformation is at the heart of his being, the itch
To create change into a new kind of seeing, which

Cannot be known if looking at garden or sky
But sensed by imagination in and of a new inner eye.

To the Moon

To come out here and sit alone.
Moon, I possess you, you are at the full.
You linger in the treetops to the west.
This at least is true. You control the tides,

Very high, very low on the coast of Maine.

I say I possess you but you possess me.
Last night you were adorable, like a woman adored,
You made the ocean quiet all over Penobscot Bay,
You gave a dreaming quality to the oceanic world.

You are a mask for the fates of mankind.

Everybody said how beautiful you were last night.
We had all heard Beethoven exclaiming, suffering.
Beethoven played to a full house in Blue Hill.
But you, white moon, were superior to him,

Your influence is beyond the human voice.

When you are at the full, making for adoration,
(Grandmother interrupted, she is agile at ninety,
Drives from Boston to the State of Maine with ease,
And has just come over to see how we are doing),

Grandmother has lived through many of your phases.

Now there is nothing to say about the moon,
A loon is calling out on misty ocean waters.
It is so calm I hear no far bell in the bay,
This poem is being destroyed by time.

Commas in Wintertime

The cold holds everything in abeyance,
The effort to find out the mystery of life,
The struggle to perceive what is perception,
The longing to pierce the truth of St. Theresa,
The belief to discover what should be belief,
The radical daring to dare at all,
The grandeur of messages from another world
While the intellect says there is no other world,
The pain of realizing another death
When we are headlong going to our own death,
Prospects of desire, thought to be illimitable,
Caught short by the failing of everybody,
Shoots of remembrance, long and oblique,
Of incredible joys lost beyond memory,
What it was like to be truly enraptured,
How the senses captured what was remarkable,
How everybody else would die, but not I,
The leap of imagination in the dark,
The grasp of self, else lost to others,
Hopeless belief in one's infallibility,
Darling ego, surge of certain selfhood,
How could the world go on without me,
One's surge love never to be recognized,
The inner secret of inscrutable events,
Soul of the world, ever to be secret,
Reality, hard and final, final, hard,
Breathe shallow, it is twenty degrees below zero,
When six I saw Halley's comet over the back fence,

Fantasy of the Impersonal

I had a fantasy of the impersonal,
That if you could get rid of the personal,
Ambitions, jealousies, paranoia,
You would be living as supremacist
Where in your ego you thought you were,
Conqueror of essence, which means death
To death, giving forth orders to life.
Let the king be a symbol of the people,
People used to have kings, now no more,
They have presidents who are relativists
Supposed to particularize amorphous people.
This kind of man or woman, no saint,
Is supposed to be impersonal not personal.
It is fantastic to think of the impersonal
When every one of our acts is personal,
When every one of our acts makes imperfection
When we fantasize about impersonal perfection.
Men invented gods in ancient Greece
To exceed themselves, but had to fail
Because they could not think of gods
Who were not like themselves, a nice dilemma,
Only God Himself could think of being God Himself.
Yet He could not think of keeping man from trouble
For once man had apple-knowledge he was free,
Thus ready to commit error and murder,
And God could not do anything about it,
But allow poets to appraise the human situation,
And thus there will be endless harm and wars,
Whether cold or hot, and endless murder,
Whether of Kennedy, King, Lennon or you,
There will be a brain full of mischance, like
Einstein's, who began the end of an innocence,
Superpowers vying whether they can kill
Each other twenty times over or thirty,
Einstein-extermination. It is all personal,
The will and ability of individual persons,

Yet I can have an evening fantasy
Of the idea of the impersonal, justice
Beyond the actualities of the individual,

Who is that impersonal god up in the sky,
Any better than I am down here below?

And why should I think of impersonal justice
When we are so rich in futility and death?

Fantasy of a Small Idea

I have a fantasy that a small idea
Is as good as a large idea, may be better.
Einstein had a large idea, but he begot
Possibly the blowing up of the human race,
So it could not be called such a good idea.
But maybe there is the little idea of love,
So little in our time as to be debased
From what the ancients thought of it as grand,
And as Freud belittled it by dissecting it,
And who with Satanic Hitlers and Stalins,
Struck great ideas of the world down
Which were announced by the ancient Chinese,
By fifth-century Greeks, and by Jesus Christ,
As well as by Mohammed and Buddha,
Maybe it is time before atomic holocaust
To fantasize that any small act of love,
Say any goodwill eye-flash to a passer-by
Is just possibly a great gain to humanity,
That to love anybody is a triumph of instinct
And if there are enough small acts of love to save us

We might outwit perhaps dream-bombing scientists,
Even take care of our planet without stabbing and killing.

A Dream

A loon's cry is a chortle from another world.
Gluts of silver, the dawn conclamant,
The ruffian band appears at our house.
Cinematographic, they move in,
Each face set in a rigid throat,
Their unity impressive and ominous.
The owners hover in an upper room.
Two knock, say they have come,
They need not say it, to destroy our house.
They break plates all over the place.
Their youthfulness and zest is mastery,
Without qualitative argument.

We do not have to argue either,
But touch relatives with quick glances.

In a room chock with swarming braggarts,
One is perhaps startled as two abreast
A column forces in with long guns vertical.
Our sin is putting rouge on our faces.
They march with marionette absolutism,
When they get in they dissolve in the ground.
The leaders are arguing at the pedestal.

I am waking in a university city,
The halls crowded with brutal faces,
Hundreds force into the large lecture,
Dr. Faction is lecturing on culture.
He cannot be seen, cannot be heard
Behind the solid mass of twisting flesh.
In an anteroom women gossip and knit.
It is said he is being transferred to Harvard
To the greatest university on the continent.

The loons are savage and absolute,
Their cries annihilate the relative.

Our house is being destroyed, the crowd
Is dancing and mounting in a high glee.
We are ashamed of an old order
Of sanity for which it is useless to contend.

I have fled to a new adjacent city.
Two men are struggling with polar bears,
Each has his polar bear in his arms
As big as a dog: each is wrestling
And wrestling his away from the other.

One denounces the other, "You know
You stole my polar bear." He accuses
With righteous anger. The other fades out.
They dissolve in an intrusive symmetry.

By me
Is a jewelled reindeer bright and tangy,
The flesh of another world inviolate,
Attached to a sledge of violent colors,
It is a reindeer taxicab. I ask,
Shall I take the reindeer taxicab
Back to the consequential city?

The past of abandoned truth fades,
The new dawn appears.

Testimony

I was going to make something of it
        But I lost the track.

The creative bright new world bright worldness
        Was there within a breath

Within a hair's breadth, a whisk of time,
        Some incredible minimal essence

I almost had the grasp of it entire,
        I leaned into fullness, meaning,

I had a glimpse of totality of experience,
        On the verge of an absolute,

Something sensed so fine as to be indefinable,
        Glimpse of godhead truth,

I was sure that it was going to be complete,
        As if my life were at stake,

A kind of state of being without resolution,
        Rich with immediacy too delicate,

It was a given sense of total selfhood
        When supreme vision was to appear,

The flash of some holy kind of instance,
        Some revelation imminent

When the elusive juice of electric spirit,
        The instant flash of knowing

Vanished from the mind with lightning speed,
        Left me at a lower rate,

In this lower state I lived alone and true
     To the vast corporeal thisness

Of thisness, each thing, each happenstance
     As solid as the world is long, and you.

Then I thought to invent inmost praise
     Of sundry matters everybody knows,

And feels of obdurate sameness, the common
     Touch that never effervesces,

Thought to praise life as it is, incomplete,
     Because praise of the highest vision,

Unattainable, glimpsed in a high moment
     Is altogether unattainable,

We are here in a ground of earth structures,
     Every day bread, workmanship,

We are beings who are held down to time,
     Amazed at a glimpse of immateriality,

We know we will exit soon and disappear,
     We had a sense of some otherwhere,

We had a sense of indefinable vastness,
     Beyond our powers to endure.

This is my testimony of that bright time
     You too may have felt sometime,

But why should this century deny me
     Capture of essence and light

When the Greeks and the Elizabethans knew them,
     Keats knew them incarnadined,

We are the materialists of the atom bombs,
      Fear seizes us in the joints,

We think a vision of immateriality
      Must have no meaning, none,

In our teeter and balance before annihilation,
      The end of us,

When it comes, when it comes, the blast,
      Destruction of the best and worst,

We wanted to look in the eye of God,
      We got six feet of radioactive sod.

The Killer

Rise up, poets, phalanx of the just,
Correct the stance of the erring man,
Be there in sunlight, take back his little shots,
Reverse the shattering camera of time.

There is the shadow of Oscar Williams,
Whom you left out of your anthology,
There is Gerard Manley Hopkins, who saw
A stippled trout, hurrahing for harvest,

Looking, saturated from the White Horse,
Dylan Thomas' world-view through the foam,
Yeats' knuckled hand move slowly, true,
Dowson will turn his back on you.

     Stand to your last, and lock him out,
     Poets, rise up, and stand in the light of day.

There goes magisterial Bridges, stately,
Long-lived, to suffer for a dying child.
They are closing ranks, are statuesque,
Thomas Hardy peers down to the Titanic,

Housman, no brute and blackguard, musing
Sardonic, himself a dying nonathlete,
A.E. fingers angels in his pocket,
James Stephens brings on a lady of the street.

They are forming for a picture of the times,
Eliot with the look of a Missourian,
Pound somehow radiating Idaho,
Frost quixotic, shifting on both feet,

Robinson Jeffers, claiming mountain, sea, and stars
Superior to the antlike crawl of man,
Hart Crane, enlarged on the Elizabethans,
Killed by ocean water, from Chagrin Falls.

There stands Edna Millay, called Vincent,
High on a hill in Camden, looking out,
Marianne Moore, pristine, in a tricorn hat,
D. H. Lawrence in a sandy-red beard, pointed,

Heavy, sun-faced Wallace Stevens, smiling,
Big-browed Muriel Rukeyser looking like the people,
Aiken battling it out with Freud,
Archibald MacLeish understood the Trojan horse.

Cummings troubled by clarity and evenness,
William Carlos Williams patting poets on the back,
Rexroth beating a drum for pacifism, eternity,
Ginsberg howling for mercy in the face of death,

Duncan, off in the hills quoting Milton,
Ferlinghetti, concerned about St. Francis of Assisi,
Corso closely, long, final on marriage,
Kees getting lost, a dropout, a cliff dropover,

They are walking in from all points now,
The poets to form themselves into a picture,
Some have come, many are left back home,
Far back in time, or in some other countries.

See, there, some of the fresh-strengthed young,
Lumbering Lowell, artful Wilbur, big-bear Roethke,
Behind them classic front-lobe Tate, vision-crested Warren,
Ransom the teacher, subtle of grammar,

Spender, who saw a high spiritual essence,
Auden, who would not flinch at the world's dirt,
MacNeice, who went for a skirt in a taxi,
Day Lewis, who wrote mysteries under another name.

They are gathering into a humane phalanx,
Each an individualist, given a gift and giving
The gift to the world of waiting takers,
Each is a discoverer, a knower, purveying truth.

Until society teaches him your worth
He will go on killing the President.

Luminosity of the aggregate poets.
If the principle of indeterminacy holds,
This poem could turn to composers or painters,
To sculptors, filmmakers, Chinese haiku inditers.

The idea is of ideal superabundance.
The world is so much greater than any man
Or woman's mind in it, greater than expectation,
That we do not wish nothingness too soon.

Think of the hard work done by Audubon,
Think of Stefansson eating only meat,
Think of Scott at the South Pole by horse,
If they had thought of dogs they would have survived.

Think of the wildness in the heart of man!
Mt. Everest does not care whether anybody climbs it,
What is a name to those eternal heights and snows.

Susan Butcher was first to climb Mt. McKinley
With dogs. My radiant niece, young woman bountiful,
Ran the Iditarod from Anchorage to Nome, a thousand miles,
Then dared, with a sixty-year-old, to seek the Guinness book.

Her sister Kate, quiet, took to Greek and Latin,
Won a Greek prize from New York University.
Abundance! Is it better to take dogs up McKinley,
Or to understand subtleties of Greek literature?

What a joy to talk about persons not in the books.
Our poetry is studded with university acclaims and notices,
Poets are elitists of an unelite democracy,
Nobody will listen to them but those in the know.

Ideal superabundance, the state of grace of the nation.
While everybody reads the savage, low-lying press,
The ecstasy of primitive, inveterate consciousness
May be inflaming a young unknown poet to greatness.

Behind the news is as big as behind the eyes.
For behind the eyes, before they become blind,
And make us weep, but dry, no tears to weep,
Behind the news is the astonishment of reality.

The heart of the nation thrives with living thrust,
The heart of this nation is extravagant and kind.
We are a people who love and hate, hope, but kill,
We are the proud inheritors of the Western world.

To talk about an individual act of assassination
Is to talk about everything, to see our splendid heights,
And our depths of depravity as one and the same,
We were revolutionists first, we still kill.

I suppose murder is as good as kissing, a terrible
Thing to say, why does anybody murder anybody
Unless because of a self-love too great to bear?
Ideal love, too, is unbearable selfhood.

I would like to have my mind range free as a bird
And I would like to be able to put down this line
Before I forget it, because I have often noted
That reality is lost if there is not pen and paper to hand.

Infallible indices, I love the idea of infallible
Indices, as if one had all of life in hand,
As if an index could be expanded to perfection,
As if the dreams of Sir Walter Raleigh were not in vain.

As if the worm, the arrow, the poison had not
Contaminated us beyond redemption by poetry,
Whose source is, was, and will be ourselves,
Our vision does not want to be obliterated.

Perhaps obliterated somewhat, so that we see
Through a gauze not plainly but with evocation,
And we have to trust the mist of the eternal veil
Between knowing and the truth of unknowing,

How does all this sort with lavish reality?
Is reality so great a thing that we think
That reality is everything? The greatest things
Are full of unreality, as Christ on the Cross.

And if poetry could make you happy
It would have to contain all pain, all misery,
It would have to be so deep in the substratum
Of your being that you would have to—what?

What word can assess the human situation,
The lyric flight of the bluebird's joy,
The awful recognition of a cancer patient's death,
The changes of life, recognition, strengths of hope.

Think of our little cinder somewhere whirling
Beyond the consciousness of man in a death
No man can understand or supervise,
Nothingness the everything we can contemplate.

What was the hope of mankind, where
The territories of love, desire, human greatness,
When language was silenced in a long darkness,
When God, inscrutable, is beyond the universe.

Here the song the poets sing,
It is the song of the ages, now.
They sing the moment of absolute good,
Piped by a piper piping.

They are to make the world anew.
It was true before, it is still true.
If winter is white, spring is green,
A spirit of being lithe and lean.

Go to the primal spring
Against killing anything.

Tick, zip, zip, tick
In the humid night air insects
Hit an electrical grid, emit
Zipping flashes big or little

As they zip off to the eternal
Flashing crispest sounds, ticks
Continuously intermittent,
Hit, flash, emitted tick

They encounter instantaneous fate
Hitting fatal electricity,
Tick, zip, zip, zip, tick.

If mankind can kill off the insects
Frisked in a flash, mankind is fated,
It is a matter of timing,
We do not make fireworks at night.

Nit, wit, tick, nit, wit,
Flick, hit, flit, wit, nit.

A little spot of grease goes splat, life
Winks off. We are thrown against a grid,
Death, the noise of our death splutters,
Instant show is over but the show goes on.

An amorphous grouping, coming into consciousness
Is the standing picture of the unarmed poets,
Who, word lovers, lovers of the real, the good, the true,
Are armed with poetry to take life seriously,

Not kill another human being. Letters
Are their bullets fired into the brain of man
To sanctify and fortify, to enrich not kill,
They are a crowd of life, a phalanx of perception,

I thought of Baudelaire, Rimbaud, Mallarmé and kin
All in one line. I had to leave a lot of people out,
The picture had to be more or less of my time,
A few decades in a total, massed world-wealth.

A gathering of the spirits. What a throng from deep down
In the beginning of consciousness from childhood on,
These makers of life were makers of masterful meanings
Recognized by total populations of the bright.

They are summoned to stand amorphous but newly real,
Each beside the other, although they may not have known
Each other, all of them bound by wisdom and by love,
Their spirits materialized in marching words of evocation,

Their messages loved by many, their lives
Whether harsh and bleak, or radiant or sunny
Studied by aspirers, the thoughtful, the knowing, those
Whose imagination mates with their imagination,

I cannot name those from fifty down, there are so many,
Nor can I see all of the forms of the mature and elders,
It is a pity but all limitations strengthen us
To perceive the vastness and greatness of what we do not know

Or own, but now I come to my austere belief,
The phalanx of these poets stands apart
At any man who aspires to kill the President,
They should aspire to read poetry instead.

Can madness be educated out of these youths,
In the future, these madmen, these killers,
Can our society tolerate their malign brains
When there is much in life they do not sense or feel.

It is improbable that they will see my picture
But we must strive to put an end to death
By gunshot, and earn deeper meanings by deeper knowings,
The offended poets, standing in a row, shot too

By ignorance, fear, and violence of the killer
Cry out against the cold, barbaric bullet intrusion,
They stand here every one giving love and belief,
Hope, courage, strength, true mortality from poetry.

    Killer, you are a man. Listen to the poets,
    Or you will go on killing the President.

Chocorua

Preface

Every time I drove past Mount Chocorua I would think of Chocorua's defiant gesture of leaping to his death from the peak after shouting maledictions at the white man. My wife had climbed the mountain many times in her youth.

In 1964 I thought of writing a verse drama about the story but soon realized how little I could find out or learn about the actual living conditions of the Indians and whites and of their social conventions. I could not flesh it out.

Then I thought to write the shortest, most compressed account of the Greek-like tragedy. I wrote the playlet not to be acted but to be read. I put it away, looked at it again in 1969 and improved it somewhat.

The plot is threefold: the death of the Indian boy by accident, not design; the revenge of the Indian father, multiple murder; the final revenge of the white man, trapping Chocorua on the mountain peak from which, rather than be shot by them, he leaped to his death. It is a true story, now a legend, but few people seem to know about it. I thought one purpose of this verse playlet would be to preserve the facts which are basically tragic in a Greek sense, the sense of inevitability and remorselessness. Another would be to express my interest in the conflict not as local, something that happened nearby, but as universal, a reminder of the tragic view of life.

SCENE I

Chocorua appears in full Indian regalia and speaks.

CHOCORUA:
We own this land and we worship the sun.
My people are strong. Swift, silent, fleet,
We outwit the animals, we kill them for meat.
We love land and mountain, we worship the sun.

The lakes are beautiful to us, the clear streams,
The great stars in the nights of summer, nights
Of quiet before the moon, when nothing fights,
And we have the courage of ancient dreams.

We worship the sun, we worship this peak,
The pointed mountain that is ever the same,
Despite weather or man, from which my name
Comes, Chocorua. Like it, my strength is harsh and bleak.

His son appears.

SON:

Father, take me to the farm in the meadow.
I want to play with the children. My friends there,
The boys and the girls they all play fair,
Let me run with them between the sun and the shadow.

CHOCORUA:

Come, son, I will take you to the white cabin.
While I hunt, play safe and be good.
If they offer it, eat the white man's food,
And do not run into any danger or sin.

S C E N E   I I

A cabin in the clearing.
John and Priscilla, and their several children. Chocorua enters.

JOHN:

Welcome, Chocorua. The day is beautiful and fair.
We are glad to see your son. I am ready to go
Far afield to plow, and to reap what I sow.
Welcome, Chocorua, let our children play without care.

CHOCORUA:
> I brought my boy because he loves your kind.
> Let them play together. I go to seek meat
> In the forests for my people to eat.
> To the stealth of my arrow the deer will be blind.

PRISCILLA:
> Chocorua, we will take good care of your son.
> While I am working, when they are hungry
> I will feed them, they shall be well fed and carefree,
> And let them play together as they have always done.

> *Chocorua departs with a salute, saying to himself:*

> My keenness of sight always looks to the peak
> Of Chocorua, as a prayer of my people, and sees
> Visions of ultimate freedom above the trees.
> It is a kind of purification that I seek.

> I took my name from a high reality.
> These ancient lands were before sin
> When they belonged only to the Indian.
> I have tried to conciliate my pride with white perfidy.

SCENE III

> *Later in the day, evening.*
> *John appears at the cabin, a scene of horror.*

PRISCILLA:
> John, the boy is dead! It is beyond belief!
> John, help me. I loved him as my own.
> I went to the fields. I left them alone.
> See, he ate rat poison! Oh, beyond belief!

JOHN:
> Chocorua will be coming any time now.

PRISCILLA:

Words are of no use. I wish I were dead.

JOHN:

I felt out in the woods a suffering in my head.

PRISCILLA:

He thought the can had jam in it, or honey, somehow.

S C E N E   I V

Chocorua appears at the cabin. His son is dead. All are grief-struck. With the stoicism of the Indian, he does not break down, but maintains an imperturbable dignity. No one could see in his deportment the motive of revenge.

Chocorua, slowly, looking upon his dead son:

Grief is too deep for any words of mine.
My shafts were true, my arrows were sharp, my soul
Delighted to kill, but now I am not whole.
At my birth fate showed an evil sign.

JOHN:

You will not believe us, Chocorua, you
Will not believe us. You will see
Betrayal in the land of the free,
Chocorua, but it is not true, O it is not true.

Chocorua with great dignity gathers the body of his dead son and walks out of the cabin.

A year later. The cabin.

JOHN:

It was a hard winter, but now this July
Bids fair to give us all the food we want
And by Thanksgiving we shall not have to scant.
The fields prosper. I am going farther afield today to try

To wrest more substance from the land. By nightfall
I shall return, be good to the children, be,
Beloved, happy and glad that you are free,
Know my hard work is for the love of you all.

PRISCILLA:

You know, John, it is ever what is unsaid,
However the children may seem happy and gay,
When I think of that summer-fatal day
That lingers darkly in my light and loving head.

Go, John, we will be secure and happy here.
The well is without tincture, and sweet-tasting.
I will take good care of the children, haste
Home by nightfall, go, John, go, my dear.

John departs.

SCENE VI

John appears at nightfall at the cabin, a scene of horror. Every member of his family has been brutally murdered.

JOHN:

Gods, grief! Chocorua! My god, my wife,
My little ones. Death! All dead, my eyes
Blinded by horror, savage cries
Leap in my throat like the sharp knife

Of vengeance, O incredible, my heart
Fails, my head reels, my speech breaks
In passion for their murdered sakes.
Unreal! I dream! I lurch, I stare, I start

Oh, no! Oh, no, Chocorua, great heart,
Do not do this to me. I rail
On fortune as all lights fail.
And I am afraid like Adam at life's start.

S C E N E   V I I

A year later at the cabin. John, with neighbors.

JOHN:

We tried to make Christian the Indian
But the ancient laws of nature are deep.
Neighbors, let us never rest or sleep
Until justice shall expiate Chocorua's sin.

We gave them love, but the law of brutality
Is deep in the hearts of us all, now seek
Redemption, to be free, in the bleak
Justice of death to Chocorua's savagery.

NEIGHBOR:

We are not rid of fear, we will join you
In posses and stratagems. We are blunt
Men and we shall search and hunt
Down Chocorua. To ourselves we must be true.

NEIGHBOR:

It is known that Chocorua, noble
Savage, seeks the mountain cliffs and height,
Serene beyond his people's troubles,
To meditate in the middle of the night.

His ways are sure and known. He takes the path
Shortest to the top, there to find
In prayer the leadership of his mind and kind.
When dawn comes we shall kill him in cold wrath.

JOHN:

I hesitate, in some dark part of me, to choose
Vengeance against our Indian enemy,
But, though blinded, no other way see
Toward justice, and am with you in any ruse.

SCENE VIII

*A scene at the top of the mountain. Chocorua, noble, savage, de-
fiant, stands at the peak, surrounded by a posse of white men be-
low the summit. It is dawn. The farmers are armed with rifles.
Chocorua holds a bow and arrow, with which he has just shot a
deer which lies on a crag below the summit.*

JOHN:

Chocorua! come down! You are surrounded.
You cannot escape. We have you in our power.
Descend, or this is your fatal hour!
At the peak you are hounded and grounded.

NEIGHBOR:

Give in. Renounce your savagery. Descend!
Our fingers itch and twitch to fire.
Chocorua! Man we have loved, higher
There is none. Give in, your people defend, defend!

*It is a tense, dramatic moment. The posse is bent on killing a de-
fenseless man and yet they have sufficient humanity to wait a mo-
ment. In that moment Chocorua takes fate into his own hands,
denounces the white race, and with a prophecy that he shall ruin
their wells and haunt their future, that his people shall be trium-
phant in the skies, with a magnificent gesture of defiance hurls
himself to death on the rocks below as he says:*

In the name of the Great Spirit I defy you,
I will never give in, you are evil,
You accomplish the works of the devil,
May your sins against my people haunt you

To the ends of the earth, throughout time,
I curse your streams and announce malediction
To your people in the wrath of my conviction,
I leap to an eternity that is my people's and mine.

Curtain